MEL RENFRO

FOREVER A COWBOY

an authorized biography by

BOB GILL

FOREWORDS BY BOB LILLY AND ROGER STAUBACH

PORTLAND • OREGON
INKWATERPRESS.COM

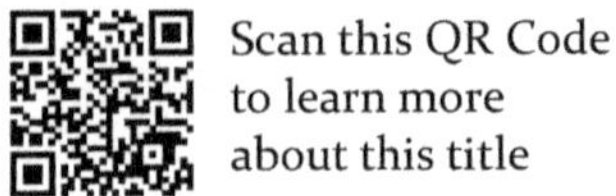

Edited by Linda Franklin
Cover and interior design by Masha Shubin
Cover photo courtesy Bob Lilly. The Dallas Cowboy star is a registered trademark of the Dallas Cowboys Football Club. Used with permission.
Back cover photo ¢ Pro Football Hall of Fame. Used with permission.
Interior photos provided with permission by: the Mel Renfro family, Eric Evans, Steve Liskey - RetroCards.net, and Robert Gill. Owners hold respective copyright.

Gill, Robert F., author.
Mel Renfro : forever a Cowboy / by Bob Gill.
pages cm
Includes bibliographical references.
LCCN 2015917057
ISBN 978-1-62901-299-5
ISBN 978-1-62901-300-8
ISBN 978-1-62901-301-5

1. Renfro, Melvin Lacey, 1941- 2. Football players--United States--Biography. 3. Professional athletes--United States--Biography. 4. Dallas Cowboys (Football team) 5. Biographies. I. Title.

GV939.R455G55 2015 796.332092
QBI15-600214

Publisher: Inkwater Press | www.inkwaterpress.com

Paperback ISBN-13 978-1-62901-299-5 | ISBN-10 1-62901-299-8
Hardback ISBN-13 978-1-62901-300-8 | ISBN-10 1-62901-300-5
Kindle ISBN-13 978-1-62901-301-5 | ISBN-10 1-62901-301-3

Printed in the U.S.A.

3 5 7 9 10 8 6 4 2

*The book is dedicated to my wife
Faith, my lifelong cheerleader.*

Contents

Foreword

After I graduated from high school in Pendleton, Oregon, and moved on to Texas Christian University in 1957, I would hear raves from the town people and my coach Don Requa about the football and track skills of a special Portland high school athlete, Mel Renfro.

Later in 1962, when I was listening to the Texas-Oregon football game on the radio, Renfro's name came up again. Even though Texas won the game, his name was repeated over and over. Mel was extraordinary on both offense and defense. Finally the announcer stated, "Mel Renfro is the greatest collegiate player I have ever seen." Mel did become a consensus All-American that year, and I was very excited when the Dallas Cowboys drafted him in the second round in 1964.

Image provided by Steve Liskey - RetroCards.net

Bob Lilly

I met Mel when he came to our training camp in Thousand Oaks, California. From the first day, I was in awe of his talent. He could run with great agility, and he was a fast learner. Although he was quiet, I gathered Mel was just listening and learning. It was an admirable trait because his football IQ and concentration set him apart.

I watched Mel move into the weak safety position and play like a veteran. He was also good in the kicking game as a punt and kick-off return man. During his Cowboy career, Mel was a top-notch valuable member of our famed "Doomsday" defense. In my opinion, Mel was the top defensive back in the entire NFL because he could play both safety and cornerback at an all-pro level every game and every year during his 14-year career.

I was thrilled when the Cowboys added Mel to their Ring of Honor in 1981, putting his name on the wall of Texas Stadium along with mine. I was also extremely happy when Mel was inducted into the Pro Football Hall of Fame in 1996. Even though Mel and I became friends early on, our friendship has grown over the years. I am very proud to call Mel Renfro my friend.

BOB LILLY, 2015

Foreword

Mel Renfro and I were Cowboy teammates for nine of my 11 seasons in the NFL. We have shared the ups and downs of the game we both loved to play – all for same coach, Tom Landry. When I joined the team in 1969, Mel was one of the best athletes I had ever known. He could have played many positions in the NFL.

Coming into professional football as a rookie was an eye opener for me. I felt I had the arm and the speed to pass and run at that level, but I found out early as a quarterback that experience is the main factor. The pro game is so sophisticated that many rookie quarterbacks aren't equipped to handle that sort of pressure and responsibility.

Image provided by Steve Liskey - RetroCards.net

Roger Staubach

Yet, when Mel came to the Cowboys in 1964 as a running back and receiver, things were different for him. Landry immediately recognized his exceptional speed and football talent. Mel needed to be on the field. The coach found a starting position for him as a defensive back and utilized him as the kick and punt returner. The rookie had a breakout season by setting team records. Mel replaced three veteran starters and earned his first Pro Bowl selection of the 10 consecutive choices he would receive.

Mel was humble and quiet, but he would always be there if you needed him. He is not only a Hall of Fame/Ring of Honor athlete but a great person and friend.

Roger Staubach, 2015

Preface

MEL RENFRO IS ONE OF THE EARLY DALLAS COWBOY LEGENDS.

As a defensive back, Mel played 14 seasons of professional football with the Cowboys, in four Super Bowls, and participated in in ten Pro Bowls. He has been honored with inductions in the Pro Football Hall of Fame and the Cowboy Ring of Honor.

Impressive, but one paragraph doesn't tell enough about Mel Renfro. He has a strong and compelling story.

As a high school quarterback at Portland's Jefferson High School in the early '50s, I played football with Mel's oldest brothers, Dallas and James. Then beginning in 1957, my freshman year in dental school, our Friday night entertainment for three years was watching Jefferson football. With Jefferson's 34-1 record, the games were awesome, and Mel's play was exciting to watch.

Mel is considered one of the best two-sport high school and college athletes to come out of the state of Oregon.

Years later as an Oregon sports historian, I recognized that Mel, at age 68, did not have a published biography to chronicle his athletic exploits and his life journey. I had a personal conviction, if I didn't get one started for him, his story wouldn't be told.

When I approached Mel with the idea in 2010, he welcomed it with open arms and with a certain seriousness that many of his experiences inside and outside of football needed to be explained.

Besides recognizing him as a great athlete, the book addresses Mel's human side, including his personal struggles and his personal account of the events that led to the exceptionally long wait before his induction into the Pro Football Hall of Fame.

Acknowledgments

THE VENTURE TO WRITE AN AUTHORIZED BIOGRAPHY FOR THE DIStant Dallas resident took hundreds of hours of research and interviews. Thus the five-year project became a labor of love for this novice writer, and by the grace of God, I've grown as a biographer. But completing Mel's story and getting it published wasn't easy; it's been hard.

I would openly acknowledge Mel for his unselfish cooperation and his frankness as the key to the book's human content. To finish when I was in the "red zone," or near the goal, I sought out my favorite writer and mentor, *Portland Tribune*'s Kerry Eggers for help. He was able to provide me with the encouragement and the vital manuscript editing as I neared the goal. I scored when I searched out the Portland publishing team at **Inkwater Press,** Sean Jones, Linda Franklin, Masha Shubin and John Williams.

Picture credits and appreciation to **Bob Lilly** for the cover picture; Photographer **Eric Evans** for Renfro's Autzen Stadium picture; **Steve Liskey of *TheCowboysGuide* and RetroCard.net** for providing images for the Doomsday players, Dick Daniels, Tom Landry, Bob Lilly and Roger Staubach; the **NFL Hall of Fame** for the back cover and HOF pictures; the **Renfro** family collection and author **Bob Gill's** collection.

I also offer a tip of the hat to others: Portland high school sports' historian John Aust, talented writers Tim Marsh and Dwight Jaynes, and my fact-checking-reader, friend Dr. R.C. "Dick" Peterson.

MEL RENFRO

Forever a Cowboy

1

Appreciated Again

EUGENE, IN OREGON'S WILLAMETTE VALLEY, WAS THE CENTER OF the football universe on an autumn Thursday in October of 2010. There was excitement in the air, a westerly breeze and an overcast sky. The late-afternoon football matchup would pit the University of Oregon Ducks against the UCLA Bruins.

Oregon was ranked number one in most national polls, the highest ever for its football team. ESPN would also carry the first experimental 3-D coverage of a football game to a national television audience.

Throughout the afternoon, the exhilaration continued. Green-and-yellow banners flew as the endless stream of cars, vans, and buses made the slow journey toward Oregon's Autzen Stadium. A festive atmosphere unfolded while the tailgate and RV communities competed for space as the parking lots filled. Many alumni and athletic-fund donors greeted each other with high-fives as they entered the cavernous Moshofsky Center for their pre-game activities and meals.

Concurrently, students flowed across the Autzen Bridge from the campus and into the stadium; the marching band played "Mighty Oregon" while the cheerleaders danced on the sidelines. As game time neared, the stadium's "sea of yellow" roared approval as their Nike-clad team, in fashionable color-of-the-week "lightning yellow" uniforms, charged the field behind the bellow of the Harley Davidson–riding Duck mascot.

A near-record home crowd of 59,372 rose to its feet to pay homage to the waving American flag as the band played the National Anthem. It was nearing time to play football, as the opposing captains readied for the coin toss.

The athletic department had made a routine of recognizing past football stars as honorary captains for their home games. An Oregon legend dressed in blue jeans and a retro green game jersey sporting the large gold numeral "20" proudly stood tall on the sideline.

Photo courtesy of Eric Evans

"Let's give Mel Renfro an Autzen Stadium welcome!" boomed the public address speaker. "Renfro was a two-time All-American at Oregon before his 14-year NFL career with the Dallas Cowboys. Welcome back...Mel Renfro."

Renfro, 68, gingerly shuffled out to the center of the artificial Field Turf playing surface. He exposed his tan bald head as he waved his Oregon logo cap while pivoting around to acknowledge the applauding fans. It meant something special to Mel Renfro and gave him an intense feeling of pleasure. Mel had not been to a home football game since his own playing days in 1963, 47 years earlier.

Mel **loved** the improved facilities on the University of Oregon campus since his days as a student athlete. "It was incredible," Mel remarked. "Autzen Stadium and the Moshofsky Center were awesome, but the new Academic Center for Athletes really caught my eye where student-athletes were meeting with their tutors and everything that was offered."

Autzen Stadium, named after philanthropist Thomas J. Autzen, opened in 1967 and has undergone several expansions, bringing it to its 59,000 capacity. Prior to 1967, the football team played only three games on campus at Hayward Field, capacity 19,000, with the higher-attended games against opponents such as Washington and USC played 110 miles north in Portland at the larger Multnomah Stadium. Athletic Director Leo Harris acquired the 90-acre site in 1950 with the money received from the 1948 Cotton Bowl. Construction of the stadium took nine months and cost approximately $2.5 million.

The Moshofsky Center is a huge indoor multi-use-practice facility adjacent to Autzen Stadium that accommodates eight of the 16 intercollegiate sports. It was named to honor former Oregon football player Ed Moshofsky (1943) and his wife Elaine, whose donation made it possible for the center to be completed in 1998.

The John E. Jaqua Academic Center for Student Athletes is state-of-the-art. The lavish center, designed to be used exclusively for the academic success of the school's 520 athletes, has been a boon for recruiting. The three-story, 40,000-square-foot ultra-modern building of artistic and environmental design, which opened in 2010, was a $41.7-million gift from Nike co-founder Phil Knight. It features 25 faculty/advising offices, a library, a computer lab with 54 stations, an auditorium, lecture rooms, 35 tutoring rooms, 40 study cubicles, a café and extensive lounge areas for reading and studying. A three-story heritage wall recognizes student-athletes' photos etched on stainless steel. Even some wooden floors are engraved to recognize the academic All-Americans.

When Mel was at Oregon a half-century earlier, juggling two

varsity sports didn't leave much time for the academic side of his college career. Except for an occasional tutor, the support was limited to "Mel, are you going to class?" and "You need to stay eligible!" comments from the coaches. As a married two-sport All-American minority student at Oregon in the early 1960s, Renfro managed a C average but did not earn a college degree. He was short more than a year of work in credits when he left for the NFL. The day before the game, Mel and Dave Wilcox, his former Oregon teammate and a 49er Pro Football Hall of Famer, toured the impressive new baseball and basketball facilities together before they were formally introduced to football coach Chip Kelly's "fast-paced" football team at the afternoon practice. On game day, they shared in the festivities with friends and others at the Moshofsky Center before watching the game with their wives from a skybox atop Autzen Stadium. Mel also had the opportunity to pay respects to the widow of his own college football coach, 94-year-old Margaret (Len) Casanova.

The trip to Eugene to visit his alma mater was fulfilling for Mel Renfro. As he returned to his Dallas home, he reflected on the campus tour and the special pre-game recognition as the honorary game captain. "It was fantastic," smiled an elated Renfro. "Every department we visited on campus was very gracious to me. I am proud of the progress made at my college. I felt very good and left the stadium with the feeling that I was appreciated all over again."

2

The Early Years

MELVIN LACEY RENFRO WAS BORN IN HOUSTON, TEXAS, ON December 30, 1941, to Dallas E. Renfro III and Edna L. Jones Renfro. He was the youngest in a family of four boys, including Dallas, James and Raye.

Mel recalls that his father grew up in Conroe, Texas, with five brothers and two sisters. His dad's mother, Mel's grandmother, was a full-blooded American Indian (tribe unknown). His mother's dad was referred to as "Pappy Jones." He told Mel he wasn't a slave, but worked on the "master's" farm.

In 1944, brother Raye's health problems prompted the Renfro family to leave the rigid segregation of the Trinity Garden ghetto of Houston to seek a better climate and life opportunity in Portland, Oregon, during World War II. "Raye had breathing problems," his mother Edna said. "And the doctor said unless we moved to a different climate, Raye might die. So we started packing right then." Though he suffered from asthma all his life, it proved to be the least of his health problems.

Since employment was flourishing in Portland due to the war effort, Mel's dad went ahead of the family. Work wouldn't be in the busy shipyards, but rather as an elevator operator at the Montgomery Ward department store in the northwest section of the city. He complemented his earnings by cleaning offices in the evenings. Within six months, the father had saved enough to send for his family.

"It was a crowded train ride with a lot of uniformed servicemen," remembered Mel about the long trip to Oregon as a three-year-old. "We boys had to sleep on the train's paper-covered floors. When we arrived, I spotted my dad as we were getting off the train. Carrying my pillow, I ran and jumped into his arms."

While Mel's father worked at the large department store, his mother Edna found work in the shipyards, allowing the family to move into the two-year old City of Vanport, which Mel would often refer to as the "projects."

Vanport existed only from 1942 to 1948. It was named for the two cities on each side of the Columbia River: Vancouver and Portland. There was a severe need for housing to support the growing shipbuilding center of the Pacific Northwest. Nine thousand apartment units were hastily constructed on 648 acres on the river's flood plain as temporary housing for the World War II shipyard workers. Industrialist Henry Kaiser imported so many people from the East and the South that he chartered special trains to carry them directly to Portland.

The apartments were created in several months, all wooden 14-unit buildings with wooden foundations. Vanport became Oregon's second largest city with a population of 42,000, the nation's largest wartime housing development. The buildings that were managed by the Portland Housing Authority came with furniture, a hot plate for cooking, an ice-box to keep food cool and neighborhood laundries. The young city had a movie theater, five schools, a police department and even a college.

Vanport also left an enduring mark on Portland's racial makeup and relations. The shipyards attracted thousands of African

Americans from the South, increasing Portland's minuscule black population of 1,900 tenfold by war's end. At a time when Portland area trade unions were segregated or excluded blacks, those working at Vanport earned double their previous earnings or more. Though it was the "Jim Crow" era, Kaiser insisted on paying blacks and whites the same pay for the same job.

There were three shifts at the ship-building plants, making Vanport a bustling 24-hour city. The Vanport Superintendent of Schools, James T. Hamilton, asserted himself while weighing in on segregating the schools for the 6,000 children being educated: "No way!" He insisted on equal opportunity for all Vanport children.

"With parents at work, the entire place was our backyard. It was a time when kids were beginning to break away," former resident Eddie Washington said. "The white and black kids made their peace, addressing racial incidents in the old-fashioned way. You would first say, 'Are we going to wrestle or box?' Usually after that we'd go play baseball...together."

The local black population peaked at 24,000 in wartime. Many headed for home when the war ended, or when they couldn't land jobs there after the war. By 1948, only an estimated 4,500 blacks remained among the 18,500 Vanport residents.

A warm and wet May of 1948 resulted in rapid snowmelt in the Cascade Mountains, causing the waters of the Columbia River to rise. By May 25, the river was eight feet over flood stage. The *Portland Tribune* summarized the Vanport flood on its 64th anniversary: "On May 30 at 4:17 p.m., a railroad embankment serving as a levy gave way, and within 45 minutes, the entire city was under several feet of water and gone for good. The rising water tumbled automobiles and swirled Vanport's wooden apartment buildings off their foundations like toy boats."

Fortunately, the Renfro family avoided the immediate tragedy of the Vanport flood. Recognizing the threat to her family, Edna took seriously the possibility that the rising Columbia River could flood the low-lying housing units in Vanport. The Renfro family quickly moved to Albina, finding a rented house on North Knott Street just two weeks before the devastating Memorial Day flood.

By 1950, Portland's black population had fallen to 9,500. Once they left temporary housing, they were squeezed into a ghetto area known as Albina in North and Northeast Portland, due to redlining and longstanding segregationist practices among some of the Portland realtors.

While in Vanport, the Renfro family was active with other black families helping form the Hughes Memorial Methodist Church. Mel's dad was a deacon under Reverend Whaley. After the flood, the ministry would continue on North Vancouver at Knott Street, before it moved to Rodney at Stanton, and finally to Failing and Williams.

About the Vanport flood, Mel recalled, "Dad, in his Model T Ford, made two to three trips back to the flooded area to pick up families. Our house was full for weeks. One family was the renowned Geneva Jones family...Steve, Nick and Roman...and all their survived belongings."

Six months later, the Renfro family bought a home at 51 NE Fargo and the four boys attended nearby Boise Grade School. The following year, in 1949, Dallas, the oldest, made his way to high school at Jefferson, a mile walk directly north. Church activities at Hughes Memorial were always big events for the family. Mel remembers the beach trips to Seaside, the Easter egg hunts at Irving Park and the Jones' "tasty donuts."

Starting in 1948, Mel attended eight years of elementary school at Boise. The school housed an encouraging faculty for Mel, such as gym teacher Stan Stanton, the future Wilson High School football coach, and a fifth-grade teacher Mrs. Lee Honeywell. Mel remembered Honeywell's encouraging words: "I see something special in you, Melvin. One day, you are going to be someone; just stay on the right path." Mel

Renfro Family Collection

The Renfro Family

never forgot her inspiring words. "Staying on the right path" became an inspiration for him as he grew into a young man.

Recalling a family crisis that bothered him, Mel recounted, "When I was nine years old, my folks sat all of us down at the kitchen table to tell us they were going to divorce. I was the only one who cried." Then he added, "But they stayed friends and were together until I went off to the Cowboys. My mother was a nurse at nearby Emanuel Hospital. Although she went to very few of my games, she was always giving me encouraging advice on school, homework and football."

"When Raye and I were young, every day we played at the nearby Knott Street Community Center under the supervision of our older brothers James and Dallas," Mel recounted. "Later, Raye and I played basketball in the Gray-Y League at the center on a team coached by the Bagley brothers. Raye was the tall center who could really jump, while I played guard."

Mel showed early leadership qualities among the neighborhood kids, always actively organizing games and teams. Said Mel, "On nice days, Cleveland McCord – my inseparable best friend – and I migrated to Williams Park, better known as Dawson Park, to play with our neighborhood buddies: Eddie Ritchey, Belletta Moore, Sonny Hair, Joe Trotter and Willie Travis.

Dawson Park, located at North Stanton and Williams Avenue, had been named after an Episcopal minister in 1921. The two-acre site was a cow pasture, then a ball field and a touring stop for traveling circuses. By the late 1940s, it functioned as an unofficial town square for the surrounding African-American community. The park was the epicenter of many political and social movements during the next 30 years. Robert F. Kennedy spoke there. Civil Rights marches began there. Today, the new Randall Children's Hospital faces it.

"We also had a fun singing group called 'The Gents,' comprised of our leader, Billy Long, Sonny, Joe, Willie and myself," recounted Mel. "We would sing rhythm and blues, the popular African-American music of the time, at the Boise Grade School assemblies."

The Renfro family's large backyard was a playground for the boys and their friends. Two hurdles, a broad jump and a high jump pit made for neighborhood fun and games. All four brothers developed early hurdle and jumping skills for high school track and field in their backyard.

"High school was an easy transition for me," said Mel. "My brothers preceded me and I fit right in. I loved it on campus." Then

Mel turned serious, remembering the classroom: "High school was a whiz, except for algebra and English." He shrugged. "I had a fear of flunking both, but my teachers saved me. They worked hard with me to get a D in algebra and a C minus in English."

When the Renfro boys began high school at Jefferson, their father was welcomed and took an active role in the previously all-white Dads Club. "Mr. Renfro," as he was often called, became a common sight sporting his yellow Dads Club jacket and patrolling the sidelines at the Friday night football games.

As a freshman, Mel was very athletic on the basketball court and had an excellent season on Andy Pienovi's freshman team. To the disappointment of the varsity basketball coach John Neeley, Mel's basketball talent wasn't utilized. He decided not to turn out. Following his first year in high school, Mel made the decision to concentrate on just football and track. "I didn't want to do all three," he said. "It seemed too much for me."

3

Jefferson High School

After the opening of the Morrison Bridge crossing the Willamette River in 1887, it was four years before East Portland and Albina were incorporated into Portland. By 1920, 120,000 lived there.

When Portland's third high school building – a four-story, E-shaped, Florentine-style structure – was erected in 1909, it was the largest of its type in the country. Jefferson was located in the North Portland Albina district on the back pastures of the William Killingsworth farm. At the time, Albina was the third self-sufficient thriving community in the city.

Hopkin Jenkins, a Yale graduate with a background as an instructor and principal, took over the helm in 1909 and personally hired most of the faculty. As a prominent and dedicated figure at Jefferson, Jenkins commanded both attention and affection. He remained at the school until 1940. The football field is named after him.

The Albina community remained unchanged for many years. Jobs provided by the shipyards during the WWII attracted large numbers of families to North Portland. Jefferson had an enrollment of 2,600 in 1943.

Later, the makeup of the Albina district changed markedly.

The major displacements were due to the 1948 Vanport flood and the 1951 Minnesota Freeway (a.k.a. Interstate Highway 5) cutting a swath through the center of the neighborhood, eliminating 200 homes. Adding to the change was the construction of the Exhibition and Recreation Center, the urban renewal displacements and the building of the Memorial Coliseum. Ten percent of the families moved east; the remainder moved north. Nearly all of the families displaced by the freeway chose not to relocate in the Jefferson attendance area. Many Albina families moved north.

Throughout the years, the school served and adjusted to the urban changes and needs of the shrinking school district. By 2014, the large school building had attendance of a mere 520 students.

Although Jefferson had a small percentage of African-American students until the 1960s, there were a few good early black athletes. Historian Herman Brahme pinpointed the earliest as Bobby Robinson, a Jeff four-sport athlete in 1924–25 who went to the University of Oregon when blacks weren't allowed in the dormitories. In 1926, when the law changed, allowing Robinson to live in the dorms, it was a momentous year for him. Robinson became the first African-American to play full-time quarterback at a major college. Bob Reynolds, a three-sport athlete at Jeff in 1940–41, also played football at Oregon, followed by big Emery Barnes, Jeff's 1947–48 three-sport All-City athlete who became an All-Coast defensive end and high jump champion at Oregon.

The high school had a rich early history of sports stars: Bobby Grayson, class of 1932, a Stanford All-American football player and a NFF Hall of Famer; Joe Gordon, class of 1933, a baseball Hall of Fame second baseman with the New York Yankees and Cleveland Indians and later a manager for Cleveland, Detroit and Kansas City; and Pro Football Hall of Famer Arnie Weinmeister, class of 1941; all got their start at Jefferson. But the peak of the Jefferson sports history arguably was the athletes and teams of the late 1950s, when their sport scene flourished led in part by players Terry Baker and the Renfro brothers.

Football

In the 1950s, the physical game of high school football was a popular team sport for boys at the North Portland school.

During the fall, the Friday night games under the lights at Jefferson were the local center of interest. Scenes featuring the blurred image of a blue and gold–clad player streaking for a touchdown – followed by the roar of the crowd and the loudspeaker barking "Touchdown, Jefferson!" – burned in the hopes and souls of many future players-to-be. It was no different for the four Renfro boys. Their interest in playing football started slowly and the skill level increased with each brother.

Without the benefit of organized programs at the public grade school level in North Portland, the game of tackle football wasn't taught until high school. Thus, most players' talent wasn't developed until their junior and senior seasons. The exception would be the youngest and the precociously talented Renfro boy.

Dallas, the oldest brother, was big and fast, but he needed to be challenged to turn out for football by the coach at a sports assembly. Due in part to getting such a late start, Dallas never mastered the game of football. But he did receive a taste of the sport by starting three games at fullback on Jefferson's 1952 city championship team.

The oldest Renfro boy enjoyed the thrill of the game and the camaraderie with his teammates. He passed it on to his brothers. Running up and down the playing field sidelines during those games were James, Raye and Melvin. They emulated the players and fantasized their own futures.

Dallas's football coach was Eric Waldorf, a former Washington State star player recruited by Hopkin Jenkins in 1928 to strengthen the Jefferson program. The authoritative and distinguished white-haired Swede, referred to by many as the "Gray Fox," finished his 23rd year at Jefferson (in 1952–53) by leading both the football and track teams to the Portland city (PIL) championships. It would be his last year at Jefferson, although he returned to high school football coaching at Forest Grove High from 1957 to 1960.

Waldorf, a member of the State of Oregon Hall of Fame, won 10 city football titles while coaching some great players, most notably Buck and Bobby Grayson, Ray Woodman, Roger Dougherty, Ben and Roy Ell, Paul Bennett, Joe Wendlick, Jake and Solly Hergert, Alan Bartholemy, Ralph Davis, Arnie Weinmeister, Floyd Simmons, Don Stanton, Walt Kelly, Emery Barnes, Monte Brethauer and Roger Williams.

Asked to accept an administrative decision to give up the track and field coaching reins, the proud Waldorf was miffed and felt disrespected. He decided to retire from coaching and enter the business world, a dry cleaning establishment in Forest Grove. His departure opened the coaching opportunity for his second-year assistant, Tom DeSylvia, who would play a strong role in the lives of the younger Renfro brothers.

Renfro family collection

DeSylvia

Tom DeSylvia, of Portuguese and Irish descent, had dark brown eyes and a coal-black crewcut. He was 5-11, stocky, muscular and strong as a grizzly. The high school football legend from Butte, Montana, played in a state championship game as a senior. "We were tough," he would brag. "We had three fights on our team that week, and I was in two of them."

After a Navy stint in WWII, he began his four-year football career at Oregon State. As a lineman, DeSylvia played in every game for the single wing–oriented Lon Stiner with the likes of Bill Austin (New York Giants) and Ken Carpenter (Cleveland Browns) for three years and for Kip Taylor his senior season. As team captain in 1949, he led the Beavers to a 7-3 record, Taylor's only winning season, while upsetting Michigan State and Oregon. Although he was drafted by the Philadelphia Eagles, DeSylvia instead began his coaching career in Portland as an assistant to Ted Ogdahl at Grant. The following year, he was transferred to Jefferson.

Due to the graduation of the senior-laden 1952 city champions, Eric Waldorf's parting comment to his successor was: "Tom, you will be fortunate to win three games next year." The 29-year-old DeSylvia, eager to make an impact on the program, was up to the challenge. His first team, with only seven returning lettermen, came out passing and scoring touchdowns. They went 6-1 in the regular season and reached the state semifinals. The high-scoring Democrats set a school scoring record, allowing DeSylvia to play a lot of juniors.

The playing time became a boon for running back James Renfro. When Mel's brother returned his senior year, he was able to play a major part in their run for the city championship. It earned James second-team All-City honors and a football scholarship to Washington State. He lettered at WSU in 1956 and 1957.

DeSylvia was a good fit for Jefferson. Turnouts for the freshman and jayvee teams almost doubled in number. Thirty-member teams of the past now pushed sixty. The new coach's enthusiasm was contagious, and his players loved to play for him. A good example was his weekly lineman and linebacker drills; although tough, they were spirited and fair. "You have to earn your spots," DeSylvia would say, "because I don't play favorites." But once you earned his praise, he would go to the mat for you. He had good instincts for coaching and his simple approach worked for him.

He chose his quarterbacks wisely, going for leader-types who were capable of calling their own plays. He also preferred seniors as starters, believing juniors would continue to improve if they were kept "hungry." This plan worked well for him for the first three years as the Democrats finished with winning records. In 1956, DeSylvia experienced the only losing season in his coaching career with a 3-5 record. It didn't sit well with him. By midseason, he was playing many underclassmen. The jayvee and the freshmen teams completed undefeated seasons. While Raye Renfro and Terry Baker led a strong jayvee team, it was reported by freshman coach Forrest Dalrymple that "the youngest Renfro tore up the freshman schedule."

"Many of DeSylvia's pre-game pep talks weren't cerebral," recalled Mel, "but they certainly appealed to the guys. With his deep voice he would snort: 'Are you guys ready?' Which he would follow with an equally passionate plea: 'Go out there, reach down as far as you can, block and tackle, and, have fun.'"

DeSylvia opened the eyes of many football people with his success. When opposing coaches underestimated him, they learned the hard way to respect his teams. Physical play and scoring touchdowns by well-coached players were good lessons. "Coach was a very caring person," remembered Mel. "He took a few of us out for a steak dinner before one of our important games. It was the first time I had dinner out at a restaurant. He was always helping out someone. He was all about community and family. He was like a second father to me."

Terry Baker – who would go on to win the Heisman Trophy as a quarterback at Oregon State – grew up without a father in the home. He had similar feelings to Renfro's about DeSylvia. "I never had a coach who cared more for me as a person and how I should develop, than merely as an athlete," Baker said. "That may only be fiction in my mind, but it's there."

Tom DeSylvia coached at Jefferson for just nine years, winning seven city championships and gaining the state playoffs eight years from 1953 to 1961 for a 74-15 win-loss record. He won the Coach of the Year award in 1958 and was inducted into the State of Oregon Sports Hall of Fame in 1997 as a coach, a testament to his winning teams. He died December 2, 2002, at the age of 78.

4

Varsity Football

IN 1957, MEL RENFRO'S GROWTH AS A FOOTBALL PLAYER EVOLVED with the rebuilding of a program that had experienced a down year. As a sophomore, he was eager to join his new teammates and learn his role at the varsity level. It could not have worked out better for his development as a premier player.

"I was excited," recalled Mel. "I loved the game and was happy with the opportunity to be on the field. Recognizing the competition, I knew I was able to compete with the big boys and play with my brother and Terry Baker."

There was a noticeable energized atmosphere in the parks of the Jefferson district that summer, whether it was Vernon, Peninsula, Overlook or Irving. The seniors, motivated to succeed, led the summer workouts.

"The Jeff Boys of Summer," authored in 2012 by team co-captain Doug White, was his 2012 essay reflection on Jefferson's 1957 season. White was the key senior leader – with a plan.

"We can do this!" charged White. "We can win games! We can win by demonstrating our best traits, as we did by winning the city titles our freshman and sophomore years."

White, with other returning lettermen Dick Howells, Mike Henselman, Sam Holteen and quarterback-apparent Dick Peterson, met almost daily at Vernon Park to pass the football, get in shape and share their visions for the coming season. They each felt their team needed better discipline and better conditioning to return as winners.

Good line play was always a trademark of a Tom DeSylvia–coached team. The 1957 team had the potential. "Our team was loaded with talent that needed to be developed," said White. "Glen Williams, Jodie Weatherall, Ray Evers, John Thies, Vic Ellis, Dennis Prozinski and sophomore Herb Washburn along with vets Howells and Holteen." Howells and White were team co-captains.

Said Peterson: "Holteen, Hanselman, Weatherall and Prozinski – the quartet DeSylvia considered the best guards in the state – battled in every Tuesday scrimmage to decide who would start on Friday night. Not only was it competitive, it became a weekly war – almost a blood bath until DeSylvia stopped it with, 'You guys are killing each other.'"

Renfro family collection

Renfro brothers

"Then there were the Renfros," offered White.

"Raye Renfro was a powerful running back," he said. "His 6-3, 190-pound size commanded the attention of opposing coaches, small linemen and defensive backs. When he wore that infamous white towel around his neck, the defenses knew: 'Here comes a fullback who will take on anyone with his high knees and a strong stiff arm.' On defense, Raye was both an intimidating and sure tackler."

Mel Renfro, a promising sophomore on the '57 squad, was also evaluated.

"Mel began to show his talents early," recounted White, "when he beat out a bruising runner in Harvey Jackson. At 5-10 and 160 pounds of muscle, Mel seemed to characterize that 'perfect player.' He was fast and elusive; he could throw and catch; he could tackle well, and always, he came up smiling. He was likeable, coachable and fun to be with."

Although Jackson, a junior, excelled as Mel's backup as a power runner, he also earned attention as a run-stopping linebacker. Jackson's tackles were collisions. Years later, DeSylvia would gloat: "Harvey Jackson was the toughest player I've ever coached."

An early change in the starting lineup proved significant. When the Jeff team opened the season with an easy 56-0 win over Madison, a lanky 6-3, 175-pound left-handed junior took over for injured senior Peterson at quarterback. His name was Terry "Butch" Baker.

"I felt badly for Peterson when his injury occurred, and I was hoping Baker could take over the quarterback duties," said White. "We all knew that he was an outstanding athlete, but we also needed someone who could command and lead us to greater accomplishments. Baker's mastery of the game came early on. I became confident with his play-calling decisions. When a play lost yards, we could count on a comeback of some sort on the ensuing downs. Furthermore, I'm sure Coach DeSylvia, on more than one occasion, told Terry, 'Go with your best instincts' or 'Do something creative this time.'"

As the Jeff team grew in experience and strength, its depth also improved. While Peterson, once recovered, joined Mel as the double safeties on defense, two multi-talented juniors, Mickey Hergert and Rance Spruill, both gained major playing time as offensive and defensive backs.

On defense, DeSylvia employed the "umbrella" made popular by New York Giant defensive coordinator Tom Landry. The 5-2-2-2 formation featured five down linemen, two inside linebackers, two outside linebackers (corners) and two safeties. For Jefferson, their defense became stifling for their opponent's offense.

"Playing against teams with bigger players accounted for the many close games the 1957 team played. We were a bunch of little guys," hedged Peterson. "We had just one player over 200 pounds – Jodie Weatherall."

The third game of the season found Lincoln star running back Paul Goddard scoring three long touchdown runs for a 19-14 half-time lead, prompting a defensive adjustment. With the linebackers focusing on holding Goddard in check, Jeff scored touchdown runs by Raye Renfro and Hergert to turn the tide 28-19.

"After that hard-fought squeaker over Lincoln," noted White, "we strengthened our resolve to get better as we rolled on to seven wins before the big showdown against our undefeated arch-rival, Grant."

The City Championship

"The Jeff-Grant game loomed big...for the city championship," said White. "An estimated 8,000 fans were on hand at Jeff's Hopkin Jenkins Field. Additional bleachers were set up in the end zones and the field was rolled to smooth the surface for better footing."

"It was quite a sight to come running onto the field before such a big crowd...a perfect Friday evening," said White, who broke his helmet face guard on the opening series of downs. "I knew then we had our work cut out for us."

The rivalry game became Jefferson's break-out game. The Democrats' talent advantage on both offense and defense became clearly evident. It was a surprise not that Jeff won, but that the score was so decisive – 51-14.

Grant came out with a strong running game and scored the first touchdown only to have Jeff answer with a Baker touchdown pass to Glen Williams. Minutes later, Mel scored from the two after his

29-yard run. As he ran into the end zone for the touchdown, there was the familiar sight of his dad, decked out in his yellow Dads Club jacket, standing behind the end zone. Dallas Renfro, the excited Renfro parent, often paced and ran the sidelines during the games. "It was absolutely great," remembered Mel, "to see Pops cheering me on."

Peterson's 51-yard interception return set up the third touchdown, with Baker taking it in from the two to take an 18-7 halftime lead.

When Raye Renfro returned the second-half kickoff for an 87-yard touchdown, it wasn't evident that Mr. Renfro could run fast enough to beat his other son to the end zone to cheer him on. But the scoreboard continued to light up. Harvey Jackson scored twice, Williams caught another touchdown pass and Baker added the eighth touchdown with a 39-yard roll-out. Mel could sense that his sophomore season was something special. "Our team was unselfish," he said. "The guys loved to play the game."

The following week, Jeff edged Washington 21-19 to complete a 9-0 league season.

The State Playoffs

The state playoffs were next for DeSylvia's team. It may have been uncharted waters for them, but not for their coach. He had been there five times before, twice as an assistant and on three occasions as the Jeff mentor. The opening game against No. 1–ranked Beaverton would be a huge test. The game at Beaverton High drew widespread interest and should have been played at spacious Multnomah Stadium.

Since the Demos were underdogs and it was a travel game, DeSylvia's preparation for the semifinal game would be important. Different field surroundings and a partisan crowd loomed large, but the coach focused on the basics.

"It should be a game decided on breaks or turnovers," preached the coach. "And we need to stop their star player Mick Sinnerud with our linebackers." "Stop Mick Sinnerud" became the theme for the game. The Beaverton running back was experiencing a terrific season and was considered the state's best player.

The game opened with Beaverton's center and future Willamette University All-American Stu Hall smacking big Jodie Weatherall on his back. It became a physical battle. Sinnerud tried the line time and time again, but was met by the sure tackling of Harvey Jackson and Raye Renfro – neutralizing the Beavers' star player. "They were just relentless hitting the poor guy," said Peterson.

"Beaverton failed to properly cover a kickoff and an alert Dick Howells recovered to set up a Jackson score," Peterson said.

Then Sam Holteen recovered another fumble that led to Howells hauling in a Baker pass for a touchdown. Ted Freeman recovered a third fumble, setting up another Baker touchdown pass to Mel Renfro. Baker finished off the scoring with a touchdown run of his own to complete the 30-6 semifinal victory. Jeff's defensive game strategy carried them into the finals.

Jeff	Opponent	
56	Madison	0
32	Cleveland	7
28	Lincoln	19
32	Wilson	7
13	Roosevelt	6
26	Benson	2
33	Franklin	7
51	Grant	14
21	Washington	19
30	Beaverton	6
12	South Salem	7
334		94

The State Championship

The Oregon High School Football Championship was an afternoon game played on a soggy Multnomah Stadium's field against the South Salem Saxons on November 30, 1957. The rain and chilly weather kept the crowd down to 6,108.

A heavy early morning rain turned into a light but persistent drizzle, which slowed the footing and held the score down for both teams. Only four Jeff backs handled the ball. But Baker, Jackson and the Renfro brothers piled up 180 muddy yards, while the southpaw Baker connected on only 3 of 12 passes for 33 yards, giving the team a total of 213. Baker's total offensive of 115 yards nearly equaled South Salem's entire output.

"The emotional level and anxiety were very high for us," said White. "We were ready to play."

Jeff's first touchdown was scored in its typical fashion. With the opening kickoff, the Democrats covered 78 yards in 12 plays for their first touchdown. Mel ripped off the two longest runs of the drive – 19 yards to the Saxon 48 and, seven plays later, for 11 yards and a first down on the Salem 19. Then Baker, on an option play, eluded tackles and corkscrewed his way into the end zone. Spruill's extra point try was wide, but Jeff led 6-0.

South Salem scored its first touchdown in the third quarter, capitalizing on a misplay by Mel. The Saxons' offense had sputtered by gaining but one yard in three tries before punting out to the Jeff 40, where Mel touched the rolling ball, allowing the Saxons' Bob Bayne to recover it. In 10 plays, South Salem slogged its way to the two-yard line. After two quarterback sneaks, Keith Burres scored. Art Krueger ran for the extra point and the Saxons gained the lead.

With Jeff trailing 7-6 at the end of the third quarter, a Spruill interception stopped a Saxon drive at midfield. It became the turning point of the game and launched the winning touchdown drive that saved Mel from the embarrassment of being the goat of the game. But the drive wasn't easy: it took the play of the game by one of the team captains combined with a determined running quarterback to succeed.

Two plays after Spruill's interception and a full ten yards behind the action, an alert Howells out-hustled five players to recover Raye Renfro's fumble, after the Jeff fullback had received a three- yard pass from Baker. South Salem coach Lee Gustafson remarked later, "That *was* the play that really hurt us. Three of our boys had a chance, but couldn't get that ball."

Jeff moved from there to score in 12 plays, but it took two tense fourth-down situations by Baker to score. On fourth-and-six, the junior signal-caller cracked the left side for the needed yardage to the 20. Later, on fourth-and-goal from the five, the Demos shifted to the single-wing formation with Baker at tailback. The deceptive runner received the snap in the power play, sliced over the right tackle, squirmed and twisted into the end zone, dragging South Salem players with him. Jeff led 12-7 after an extra-point pass to Glen Williams fell incomplete, leaving 5:55 on the clock.

The Demos' stout defense, led by White, stiffened again, allowing the Saxons but 15 net yards and one first down in eight plays. On the exchange of downs, the Jeff offense consumed all but 10 seconds on the clock after four running plays. It allowed South Salem one last play, a wayward desperation pass. Jefferson had won its first 3A State Championship in football.

"Following the game inside the Multnomah Club locker room, the smell of wet jerseys filled the air," remembered White. "There was lots of screaming and yelling, shouts of victory, feelings that we did it. There was back-slapping, hugging one another...as teammates, we had accomplished our goals."

The Jeff Boys of Summer had come full circle. The senior leaders had realized their dreams by capping an 11-0 season with a state title, while the younger players looked ahead to the next season.

While Baker and White earned All-State honors, Mel was relieved by the comeback win. He gained a tremendous amount of experience for a sophomore, playing in such a hard-fought game. He also gained 38 yards on six carries.

"Plaudits to Tom DeSylvia, Terry Baker, and the rest of the state champion Jefferson Demos for proving that Portland football isn't third-rate after all," reported the *Oregon Journal*'s George Pasero. "And to Lee Gustafson and his South Salem Saxons for putting up one fiery defensive stand after another in the face of a tough, talented Jeff team."

While Raye had a league-dominating break-out year with 11 touchdowns, Mel was able to shine in his brother's shadow by scoring seven touchdowns himself. On defense, he became a force at safety. Mel's quickness and speed gave him the ability to cover receivers and make open-field tackles – a strength that would one day be his legacy.

5

The Nation's Best High School Team

"The 1958 season was the most fun I had in football," said Mel Renfro. "We came back that year with all the confidence in the world. We were faster, bigger and stronger. We had more depth, too. We just went out and had a lot of fun. It was great."

All-State quarterback Terry Baker and the Renfro brothers would lead, arguably, the best backfield in Oregon prep history. After senior-to-be Harvey Jackson took a matrimonial leave of school, tough and football-smart Mickey Hergert stepped up to complement the talented backfield group. Speedy Rance Spruill excelled as a football player and saw major playing time. He also took over the placekicking duties, a weakness of the previous season.

The offensive line shaped up well, too. Big Bill Hartman replaced Doug White at center, and a stronger Dennis Prozinski came into his own. Hard working Ancil Nance earned his way as a starter, while veteran tackles Ray Evers and big John Theis were the strength at that position. Junior Herb Washburn, a matured regular from the previous season, and the athletic Vic Ellis manned the end positions.

Although the '50s and '60s was an era of good athletes in the 10-member Portland Interscholastic League, the Democrats' advantage of having so many elite players elevated them to another level. It may be an understatement to say that Jefferson resembled a small-college team.

"It was remarkable how well Coach Tom DeSylvia handled the team's playing time, with substitutions and all," said Mel. "He was able to play a lot of kids. We had great practices – productive, but not long."

Team spirit and self-discipline were also important during those winning years. Few athletes were willing to risk misbehaving themselves out of the lineup on a Friday night. "We got swept up in the sports thing," said Baker. "And to be part of it was special. It never occurred to us to go out and do something to screw it up."

1958 Jeff Team

- Led the nation with 4,989 total yards.
- Set the state scoring record for 12 games with 512 points, 42.6 points per game.
- Shattered the PIL nine-game scoring record with 417 points and compiled 18 straight wins over a two-year period.

Renfro family collection

Terry Baker and Raye

Raye Renfro scored a PIL-record 145 points. He finished with 1,401 yards on 145 carries for a 9.7-yard average, scoring 28 TDs and an extra point for 169 points. Four TDs were passes from Baker.

Terry Baker completed 60 of 96 passes for 62.5%, netting 1,261 yards and 19 TDs. On the ground he gained 437 yards on 71 carries for a 6.2-yard average and four TDs. His total offensive net was 1,698 yards.

Mel Renfro was next with 711 yards on 66 carries, a 10.8-yard average. He accounted for 19 touchdowns – nine rushing, seven receptions from Baker, two passes and a 65-yard interception.

Rance Spruill booted 45 PATs, rushed for 257 yards for an 11.7 yard average while scoring 69 points.

Jeff	Opponent	
34	Lincoln	20
47	Roosevelt	0
45	Wilson	12
48	Washington	0
69	Grant	0
41	Madison	0
46	Franklin	6
54	Benson	0
31	Cleveland	0
41	Wy'east	6
38	West Linn	0
21	Medford	7
512		51

City Championship Season

The opening game of the 1958 season for the defending state champions was played on a Saturday afternoon on the Jeff field against a tough Lincoln squad. It was a dazzling display of offense by both teams. Jeff, led by Baker's passing and Raye Renfro's three touchdowns, scored 34 points.

Mel had an outstanding game as a receiver, catching a 30-yard Baker pass for a 50-yard touchdown with just nine seconds remaining in the first half. In the third quarter, he followed with a 47-yard reception to set up a fourth score. An imposing picture of Raye appeared in *The Oregonian* leading interference for his brother.

But the Democrats gave up 20 points to the scrappy Lincoln team, paced by their quarterback Kenny Scales and end George Spencer. The three scores were the most given up by the Demos **all** season. From that game forward, the Jeff defense tightened, allowing a mere 31 points the remaining 11 games.

Seven-game Record

An interesting media-created sidelight for the season was the scoring competition between Raye and Cleveland's workhorse back, Norm Patera – whose brother, Jack, later gained fame as head coach of the Seattle Seahawks. The newspaper reporting heated up the discussion after six games when Norm Patera, who carried the ball 30 to 40 times a game, was closing in on Bobby Grayson's 1931 seven-game mark of 117 points. In the seventh game against Benson, Patera scored 19 points to break it by one point. Raye Renfro got caught up in the media fray to the detriment of the opponents. In the seventh game, against Franklin, Raye had his best scoring effort with five touchdowns, but his 115 points total fell three shy of Patera.

Mel joined his brother's media hype to break the insignificant seven-game record (when there were now nine league games). In an unselfish display of brotherly love, he ended one of his long runs against Franklin by running out of bounds at the one-yard line. It allowed Raye to score his last touchdown.

Nine-game Record

The final league win of the season over Cleveland, a 31-0 shutout, left retiring coach Hub Shovlin with a testimonial to the Jeff team. "I knew they might slip away for a couple of easy touchdowns, but I didn't think they were **that** explosive," he said. Raye scored once to break Paul Goddard's 1957 nine-game record of 118, by rolling up 145 points, well ahead of Patera's 124.

After a Cleveland-ball-controlled first quarter, it was Mel's game to shine. He broke over left guard and raced untouched for a 74-yard touchdown. Then before halftime, Mel caught a pass from Baker in the left flat, and after two steps, he made a lateral pass to Raye, swinging wide behind him. But Raye fumbled. Mel scooped up the loose football and raced 47 yards to the Cleveland 12, where Baker completed a pass to Washburn for the score.

Jefferson rolled through the nine PIL games with ease, averaging 46.3 points per game going into the state playoffs. When the talented backfield exploded for early scores, it allowed DeSylvia to substitute freely. He played 10 offensive backs, and seven averaged more than 10 yards per try. An *Oregonian* story noted that "The Jeff team was far more than a team of a few stars. It was a heavily talented, well-coached machine with the ability to rip off yardage and score while its top stars were sitting on the bench."

On offense, the Demos fumbled only three times in nine games, losing the ball but twice. Raye was the leading ground-gainer with 1,052 yards on 90 carries. Mel carried 47 times for 607 yards and scored 78 points. Combined with Raye's 145, the Renfro brothers totaled 223 points. Baker set three PIL passing records with 1,043 yards on 49 of 76 passes for 16 TDs. Placekicker Spruill knocked through 36 of 48 conversions.

The defensive statistics during the PIL, compiled by Jeff student Jack Gilbert, were equally impressive. On defense, the Demos limited their foes to a meager 4.8 points per game. Dennis Prozinski, a future University of Oregon lineman, led the team with 124 tackles and four blocked kicks. John Theis had 94 tackles and Ancil Nance had 60. Jeff took the ball from opponents 33 times with 15 interceptions and 18 fumbles.

Quarters – Wy'east

As Jefferson senior student Art Eckman (future sports radio and TV great), a fledging sportscaster at the time, carried the KBPS broadcast from Wy'east High School of Odell back to Portland for the Friday night game, coach Don Hosford's Golden Eagles didn't know what to expect from their opponents.

Jeff scored three lightning-quick touchdowns in the first quarter in 11 decisive plays. Raye Renfro ripped off a 35-yard run for the first, then after a Wy'east fumble on the next play, Rance Spruill ran it in from the 27. Mel Renfro finished up the first quarter scoring on a 10-yard Baker pass after having two other touchdowns in the same series called back due to penalties. After Raye raced 48 yards for another score early in the second quarter, coach DeSylvia ran in the reserves. It was 34-0 at halftime.

In the 41-6 victory, the Demos amassed 231 yards on the ground and another 113 in the air for a total of 344, while limiting Wy'east to 87 yards. Raye Renfro netted 135 yards on nine carries.

In other playoff games, while West Linn edged Astoria 14-9, Medford came away with a 7-0 victory.

Semis – West Linn

DeSylvia's team spent a hard week preparing for the touted West Linn passing attack. The coach, worrying about a team let-down, ramped up his vocal intensity. Prepared and focused, Jeff took on a Lion team that hadn't given up a first quarter touchdown the whole year.

As the overflow crowd of 8,000 was getting seated on the Madison field, the Demos exploded with another three lightning-quick touchdowns within the first five minutes of the game. Mel scored on a spectacular 54-yard TD pass from Baker, Raye followed with a 70-yard run down the sidelines and Mel intercepted West Linn's Gary

Comegys's pass on the Jeff 35, reversed his field once and returned it 65 yards untouched for his second touchdown of the night.

In the third quarter, after Raye had scored his second TD, the lone West Linn drive to the Jeff 16 was halted when Spruill intercepted a pass at the one-yard line. On the return of his 99-yard touchdown, he broke stride at midfield in an unusual move in front of DeSylvia and yelled, "The game is in hand, coach!"

Penalties also erased two long Jeff touchdowns runs in the fourth quarter: Mel broke away 52 yards on what appeared to be his third touchdown, and later Spruill's 56-yard romp.

Subbing at quarterback with the backups in the fourth quarter, Mel threw a touchdown pass to Willie Travis for a one-yard touchdown to complete the semifinal game scoring, 38-0.

Medford beat Pendleton 27-26 in a thriller in southern Oregon in the other semi game.

The State Championship

When the high-scoring Jefferson team had to defend its 3A state championship against Medford, the Friday night game at Multnomah Stadium became the toughest test of the year. The Black Tornado, the undefeated team with one tie, was coached by the legendary Fred Spiegelberg. They were stifling defensively, having but two opponents score on them in 10 games.

The Friday *Oregonian* sports banner headline featured the Jeff-title defense game. The photo below showed Medford's biggest players, while back on page 4 was an elaborate spread of the Jeff team. Individual pictures of Baker, Raye and Mel together with supporting stories and stats detailed their season's march to their second championship game.

On paper, the game's advantage was clearly with Jefferson's offensive speed, size, and experience, led by the passing and running of their All-State quarterback. Even though the stingy defense of Medford allowed only a meager 3.3 points per game, Jeff allowed but 4. The Medford single-wing offense would need to score too.

But the Tornado came to play. First, they needed to slow down the Renfro brothers and somehow outscore the highest-scoring team in the nation. It forced DeSylvia to play his regulars the entire game.

The 13,874 wind-chilled fans were hardly seated when Medford sprinter Dan Peek returned the opening kickoff 55 yards before Mickey Hergert crashed through three blockers to make a touchdown-saving tackle. It became one of the game's heroic plays.

It took a total team effort to beat Medford. Terry Baker's vaunted passing game was blunted after a tackle. "Some guy grabbed my arm and just about pulled it off," remembered Baker. He was able to complete only four of his six passes for 59 yards and a touchdown before turning to the team's relentless running game. Hergert opened the scoring with a 16-yard trap play up the center, but the Renfro brothers, who had amassed 45 touchdowns between them, went scoreless.

Raye gained 75 yards on 15 carries, Mel gained 64 yards on 13 carries and Baker added 91 yards on his 13 carries. The Jefferson All-State quarterback recounted that the "belly series" offense – in which he either pitched to one of the Renfros or kept the ball himself for an off-tackle slice – was the big factor in the 16-play third quarter drive that eventually led to his scoring the vital second touchdown.

A Terry Wong fumble recovery led to a short Baker-to-Washburn touchdown pass. That score, together with a another touchdown-saving tackle by Hergert on the ensuing kickoff, sealed the 21-7 win for Jeff's second undefeated season and their second consecutive Oregon State 3A Championship.

"I'll say it was our toughest game of the year," emphatically claimed a weary Mel Renfro. "Man, they've got a defense." It became a memory that would resurface for Mel his senior season.

Meanwhile in the locker room, DeSylvia responded to questions for the following year. "Starters Mel Renfro and Herb Washburn will be back, but there will be a lot of rebuilding next year," he offered with a big smile.

Oregon State coach Tommy Prothro was quoted as saying, **"It was the best high school game I've seen in Oregon."** Prothro, known for his evaluation of talented football players, would eventually reap huge benefits from one of the Jeff stars.

Five Jefferson players were placed on the 1958 All-State team – Baker, Raye and Mel Renfro, John Theis and Dennis Prozinski.

Baker was the MVP of the 1959 Shrine All-Star classic, while Hergert, the leading rusher and pass receiver, was selected the game's outstanding back.

Later Reflections

In June 2006, before Terry Baker was inducted into the National High School Hall of Fame in Orlando, Florida, *Portland Tribune* sportswriter Kerry Eggers wrote: "It's been, gosh, nearly a half century now. But the memories of his time at Jefferson High in the late '50s still warm the heart of the first Heisman Trophy winner in the West."

"It was one of the best times of my life," said Baker, then 65. "If college was good to me, high school was great. Jefferson was known as the School of Champions." Baker reflected, "We won the state championship my last two years and in baseball my senior year, and we won the city basketball title my senior year. We won track, wrestling and golf – even the Rose Festival Queen. It was an amazing time at an amazing school."

At a 2011 gathering to honor Mel Renfro, Baker reflected on his former high school teammate and what it meant playing together: "Mel was the consummate team player. Even though he was an athletic specimen, he seemed to have a very good work ethic giving one hundred percent effort in practice all the time. Anything you asked Mel to do as a player, he would do. He'd never bat an eye or complain or let someone else do it. That sticks in my mind. He was a quiet guy, and he never promoted himself. He was one of the most unselfish players I've ever met. There was very little 'me.'"

Then in closing, Baker directed his comments at his smiling friend: "As a teammate and pass receiver, Mel, you made me a good quarterback."

The 1958 season passing records bear the comment out. Baker completed 60 passes for 1,261 yards and 19 touchdowns. With Mel's speed, he was able to separate from the defender and receive a high percentage of the passes thrown to him, seven for touchdowns. Six of them went for between 20 and 54 yards.

The 1958 team had 19 members who played some college football. Four were college All-Americans – Terry and Mel at the NCAA level, plus Hergert and Hartman at the NAIA level.

Mickey Hergert

Hergert was a late recruit to the University of Washington as a defensive back, but after two weeks of practice, he transferred to Lewis and Clark College to play offense. As a senior in 1963, Hergert led the nation in rushing and led the Pioneers to an undefeated season, earning him first-team NAIA All-American. Coach Joe Huston called Hergert, "the greatest back I've ever coached." In four seasons, he gained 3,598 yards (104 short of the then national record despite the cancellation of his last game). Hergert scored 266 points – career conference and school records that stood for 30 years.

Bill Hartman

Big center Bill Hartman was the senior team captain at Willamette University in 1962. He started 38 straight games for the Bearcats, earned second-team NAIA All-American honors and was named All-Northwest Conference three times.

Raye Renfro

In 1958, the team's most productive player was Raye Renfro. In track, he was the state 3A 100-yard dash champion. In football, he played on both sides of the ball. As a ball carrier, he had no match, gaining 1,401 yards on 145 carries for an impressive 9.7-yard average while scoring 28 touchdowns, including four receptions from Baker. Raye's 169 points broke the state record. As a linebacker, his talent was recognized by college coaches as a top run-stopping tackler blessed with size and speed. Said DeSylvia: "One of the best I've ever had."

Raye became the most sought-after black athlete in Oregon. Notre Dame, USC, UCLA, Washington and Oregon took notice. Recruiters wore a path to DeSylvia's gym office.

Although he was 18 months older, Raye became an outstanding backfield combination with Mel. Their football success was unparalleled for two seasons. But, as true for many brothers, their lives off the field took different directions. They were both competitive and good teammates, but they were independent of each other. "We didn't pal around with each other or even work out together," reflected Mel. "We had different friends."

The personable older brother's path led him into trouble off the field. He had worked at odd jobs at the Egyptian movie theater on Union Avenue to earn money to buy a used car. And, of course, a car always attracted many friends.

Mark Kirchmeier's article in the *Willamette Week* in 1982 recounted the series of events best: "Unfortunately, Raye Renfro listened to his friends. He listened to them when he and another high school athlete ran out of gas on the evening of February 15, 1959, and the friend was caught siphoning gas out of another car.

'It wasn't my car. I should have left, but I just stuck around,' Raye said at the time. It cost him a $10 fine in municipal court, but, most importantly it began to get him a reputation.

"His rap sheet grew a month later when he and some friends, cruising in his car, stopped at a gas station on North Interstate. While the attendant was not looking, one of the kids in the group threw two tires across a hedge into an adjoining parking lot where he could pick them up later. As Raye's car pulled out of the station, the kid told him what he had done. Though Raye hadn't stolen anything, Portland Police called it grand larceny...they reduced the charge to petty larceny, supposedly a 90-day sentence." But as Mel corrected later: "No! Dad went down the next day and brought Raye home."

By that time, the damage was done. Word got out that Raye was a troublemaker. The managers of the summer's Shrine football game, the showcase of Oregon's high school talent, abruptly dropped him off the team. The aforementioned incident suggested "problem athlete." The colleges where he qualified scholastically backed off.

Raye enrolled at Columbia Basin Junior College in Pasco, Washington, for a year, in hopes of getting his grades up and returning to the big-time football scene. But it didn't work out that way. His enrolled classes weren't transferable, as the Columbia Basin coaches had implied they would be. Following the junior college transcript nightmare, Raye became despondent, wanting nothing to do with football for two years. It was a mistake. His physical skills declined. He made a couple more efforts to gain traction and attention by playing linebacker at Portland State College in 1962 for his former high school coach, DeSylvia, who by that time had moved on to the college level. The single college season and an additional season with the semi-pro Portland Thunderbirds didn't translate into a pro football opportunity.

Always looking for promising free-agent prospects, the Cowboys' Gil Brandt critiqued Mel's brother. "I worked Raye out at a high school field in Portland," related Brandt in a 2012 interview. "He was rusty and out of shape."

At 26, Raye was married and seemed too old to develop his skills. "Raye's not having a true major college background hurt him," Mel said. "It was just his last hurrah."

Life ended on an operating table at Portland's Emanuel Hospital in 1978 for Raye Renfro at 38. He died of complications of diabetes and a pancreatic tumor. "Raye wasn't a bad kid by any means," Baker said. "He had as much talent as Mel and I did, and you could certainly see how his life could have gone differently. Everyone gets good and bad breaks, but Raye kept getting bad breaks – until the very end."

6

The Senior Season

THE 1959 FOOTBALL SEASON PROVED A CHALLENGE FOR HEAD COACH Tom DeSylvia: how to maximize Mel Renfro's talents? He moved his All-State halfback to quarterback and gave him the kicking duties. Knowing he would have to carry the load his senior season, Mel agreed.

Renfro Family Collection

Oregon Journal promo for Mel's senior season

"I welcomed playing quarterback my senior year with open arms," remembered Mel. "It wasn't difficult at all. I played quarterback my freshman year and appreciated the leadership role again. Even in grade school, I was always the team captain when putting teams together. I couldn't believe how many running touchdowns I made that season. Several games were like track meets. I think I scored five touchdowns in one game alone. Although I wasn't the best, I could pass the football."

Renfro's senior year was special. Not since the days of Bobby Grayson had one player so dominated the Oregon high school gridiron. The move to quarterback helped develop his versatility. Besides playing safety and outside linebacker on defense, he called plays, ran, passed, punted and kicked his Jeff team to its third consecutive PIL championship and third 3A Oregon State Championship game while extending the win streak to 34.

Renfro was not a one-man team. He was surrounded by many good players, including 1958 All-City end Herb Washburn, who also returned for his third season. Harvey Jackson, the tough runner and hard-tackling linebacker from the 1957 champions, returned after his year's absence. Speedy halfbacks Mike Barnes, George Brown, and Ron Martin joined fullback Leon Broadous and backup quarterback Ron Hergert. In addition, football and track star Mike Wyborney, a married transfer from Vancouver who sought athletic eligibility in Portland, increased Jefferson's football and track talent.

Three players donned their older brothers' jersey numbers. Even though Mel called the change to #37 a "sentimental" expression, it was actually Mel's statement of protest of how unfairly he felt his older brother Raye was treated following the petty larceny misdemeanor charge the preceding winter. "Everyone turned their back on him," said Mel.

Jim White took Doug's jersey #41, while Ron Hergert grabbed his brother Mickey's #29.

- Ken Kearney, Dick Nelson, Dick Brooks, Jack Potticary, Herb Hermann, John Anderson and Lee Eilertson anchored the line. The defense, called the "Animals" for their toughness, held 11 opponents to a mere 47 points, and yielded a record-low 33 points to the nine PIL opponents.

- The Jeff juggernaut, with Mel Renfro in command, unleashed an awesome nine-touchdown barrage to completely overwhelm Roosevelt 59-0. Renfro completed five of six passes, three for touchdowns while Jackson scored twice.
- After spotting Grant a 7-6 lead, the Demos exploded for three quick second-period TDs and went on to beat Grant 38-7 in a mud-splattered game. Renfro, Barnes and Martin scored two TDs apiece.
- Renfro, unbothered by rain and mud, ran and plunged for five TDs and added eight conversions for a PIL single game scoring record of 38 points to propel Jeff to a 69-0 conquest of Cleveland, passing Bob Beckner of Benson's 31 points in 1943.
- The Democrats scored their 27th consecutive victory to break Grant's record streak. Renfro ran for "only" three TDs, but passed for a fourth and kicked four extra points, as they smothered Washington 47-0. Martin scored twice.
- Wilson held a hard-earned 13-2 lead through three quarters before Renfro connected on a 53-yard pass play to Jackson to secure the third Demo score in the final quarter to win 20-13.
- Jeff rebounded with a decisive 26-7 win over Benson for their 29th straight win while future opponent Lincoln continued their winning ways with a 6-0 unbeaten record. Barnes, Martin, Jackson and Renfro scored TDs. Mel carried for 95 on six ground plays and added 74 through the air.
- In smothering Franklin 64-0, Renfro romped for four Jeff TDs before an ankle sprain benched him. Broadous scored three TDs and Brown scored two.
- The Demos turned back Madison 27-6, setting up the final league showdown with Lincoln. Barnes scored two TDs.

City Championship

Even though the Democrats dominated their first eight games, they had to win their last league game against an undefeated Lincoln team to claim their third consecutive PIL championship. Mel remembers the talk: "We were playing the sophisticated boys from uptown who lived in the high rises and had their parents drop them off in front of the school." In a strategic move to face the Cardinals, DeSylvia moved Mel back to his familiar position at left halfback and inserted the improved Ron Hergert at quarterback for a stronger running game.

The game was a suspenseful and hard-fought battle played at Lincoln's field in front of 7,500 fans. The home team controlled the first half, but couldn't score when its initial drive was stopped six inches from the goal line by the rigid Jeff defense.

After halftime, a Jeff drive ended with a Renfro fumble. "I was in tears," said Mel. "It was my first fumble in three years of football."

But the Democrats' offense recovered with lightning speed. From their own 10, they scored in four plays, culminating when Barnes broke off tackle and raced 68 yards untouched for the winning touchdown. Mel's defensive play and his 148 yards on 14 carries on offense helped his team keep Lincoln out of the end zone and preserve the 7-0 win, their 32nd consecutive win. It broke the 31-year-old record win streak of 31 games posted by Medford from 1925 to 1928.

Mel scored 20 touchdowns and 19 PATs his senior year for a total of 139 points, including a record 38 in a game against Cleveland, which boosted his scoring to a **career PIL record of 285 points** in three years of varsity football.

Washburn, Kearney, Barnes and Renfro earned All-City honors.

Jeff	Opponent	
59	Roosevelt	0
38	Grant	7
69	Cleveland	0
47	Washington	0
27	Wilson	13

Jeff	Opponent	
26	Benson	7
64	Franklin	0
27	Madison	6
7	Lincoln	0
70	Sandy	7
33	David Douglas	0
6	Medford	7
466		47

The Playoffs

Sandy

The quarterfinal game played on a frigid night in Sandy created an early "bump" for Jeff. After the Democrats had scored three quick touchdowns, Sandy scored their first touchdown to pull the game to 20-7. The Pioneer players were all jumping up and down shouting to themselves: "We can beat these guys! We can beat these guys!"

But Sandy's coach George Potter, the father of current Jesuit coach Ken Potter, became concerned when he looked across the field to the Jeff sideline. "I could see DeSylvia chewing out his team – that SOB," he said. "We didn't make another first down the rest of the game." The final score was 70-7.

David Douglas

The *Journal*'s George Pasero wrote of the semi-final game: "'Mel the Marvel' Renfro led the charge that swept aside challenger David Douglas before 4300 rain-swept fans in the Scots' stadium."

A first-quarter punt return in the 33-0 win on the soggy David Douglas field personified Mel's speed and elusive running style. The run was amazing. Mel ran from one sideline to other, all the while side-stepping past and evading tacklers, to complete a 79-yard score. Many of the Douglas defenders made two and three futile attempts to stop him, or even touch him. It was estimated Mel ran over 130 yards on the single play.

Return Championship Game with Medford

Having scored 103 points with little opposition in the first two playoff games, the Jeff team may have been overconfident heading into the championship game. But Mel's memories of the big games caused him anxiety and concern.

"My mother was always there. I would come home after a game and chat," said Mel. "I was very nervous before the Medford game. I remember how tough Medford was the year before, and this year we didn't have my older brother, Terry Baker or John Theis. But my mother encouraged me: 'Just go out there, Melvin, and do what you need to do, and everything will be alright.'"

On Friday night November 27, 1959, the Oregon 3A Championship game attracted 21,512 at Multnomah Stadium. It was the largest crowd **ever** to watch a high school game in Oregon. The attraction was Mel Renfro and a high-scoring Jefferson team in almost a replay of the previous year's championship game with the strong Medford team from southern Oregon.

The teams' records were well-matched. They both sported undefeated 11-0 records, had similar high-scoring offenses and tough and stingy defenses. The Black Tornado had scored 465 and allowed but 72 points, whereas the Democrats had scored 460 points while surrendering only 40 points. It also measured the coaching wits of Fred Spiegelberg and DeSylvia for a second time.

Sure enough, the fans were witness to a great high school football game. The game was a low-scoring, hard-hitting defensive battle throughout. Both teams were stopped many times between the 20-yard lines. Except for a play or two, the game may have ended in a tie or a one-point game either way. The final wrap-up and score proved it. With revenge also a factor, the tough Medford team handed Mel and his Jeff teammates their only loss in three years, 7-6.

The play of the game, although controversial, was spectacular. Fielding a fourth-quarter Jeff punt on his own 23-yard line, future Stanford player Dick Ragsdale handed the ball off on a reverse to Ken Durkee before he was about to be tackled, and he scooted down the right sideline. With the aid of a huge block by Lowell Dean to take out three Jeff players in front of the Demos' bench, Durkee scampered 77 yards for Medford's lone touchdown. The block caused a protest with the officials. DeSylvia claimed vehemently, but to no avail, that Mel was clipped before he was about to make the tackle. According to assistant coach Bob Hull, "The sideline official, Jerry Laurens, was standing in front of me. He reached for his flag, but refused to throw it."

Jeff responded with an opportunity to even the score. Mel heaved a long pass to Washburn late in the game for a 70-yard touchdown. It brought the Demos to within a point of tying the game.

"Mel had the respect of all of his teammates," said Washburn in a 2012 interview as he recreated the play. "If certain plays weren't working, he had the ability to improvise, and it always seemed to work. We were behind going into the last few minutes, so he decided to run me on a pass play – down and in. Since I needed extra time to get down the field, everyone had to hold their blocks an extra three counts." It worked. Washburn hauled in the long pass, bringing the score to 7-6.

"Coach DeSylvia decided to run for the extra point," said Mel. "We started our 'belly-series' play, but the Medford defensive line charged through to take away the first option. It caused panic. Harve Jackson wanted to score. He recklessly grabbed the ball out of my hands and hit the wrong hole, taking away my option of pitching to our trailing back Ron Martin for what would have been an easy score. We lost."

It was a heartbreaker for Jeff, even though they outgained Medford by 108 yards. The Demos' three-season win-loss record was 34-1, and both Washburn and Mel made the 1959 All-State football team. Mel also added the Wigwam All-American honor to his list.

The student newspaper, the *Jeffersonian*, reported: "It was also a night to be proud of the sportsmanship exhibited by the praying band of humble football players in the locker room." To add to the scene, DeSylvia spoke to his players, who listened in utter silence: "Men, we were just plain beaten! It's probably worse for Mel. He's never lost a game since he has played football. Now he knows what it's like to lose. I think he'll be a better man for it."

It may have humbling for Mel to lose his last high school football game, but he never lost his competitive edge. It didn't deter him. In his focused manner, the physically gifted athlete worked hard to improve his skill-sets in both track and football. Mel's incredible senior track season and his MVP Shrine High School All-Star Game performance are a testimony to that.

7

High School Track

As with football, Mel was a superb track athlete. Multi-talented, he could hurdle, jump high and far, and run like a deer. His older brothers, Dallas, James, and Raye, were all hurdlers and broad (long) jumpers, so after imitating them in the family backyard, he took to those events early. As a freshman, competing on the junior varsity level, Mel set all the school hurdle and long jumping records. As a sophomore in 1958, he stepped up to the varsity to compete with the best on the relay teams. Then as a junior and senior, he became the best.

Raye, the state 100 champion in 1958, refused to race against his younger sibling. Raye realized in his heart Mel was someone special and would rise to that occasion. He never gave Mel the opportunity.

Mel's track resume was off the charts. It was versatile and resembled a future decathlon champion-in-the-making. If it hadn't been for his love for playing the game of football, Mel Renfro may have been an Olympic decathlon medalist.

Three Years – Three Track Coaches

Bill Sorsby, a former assistant under Oregon's Bill Bowerman, was the 1958 Jeff track coach. He was followed by Horst Rickard in 1959 and Merlin "Bud" White in 1960.

Nine Track Trophies

Mel took part in nine of the track team championship trophies that adorn the glass cases in the halls of Jefferson High. Three consecutive Hayward Relay wins in 1959 retired the big trophy. The three PIL relay titles, the two PIL championships and the 1960 3A Oregon State track title complete the list of hardware.

Jeff won its fourth consecutive PIL City Relays in 1959, Mel's junior year.

- Record-setting shuttle hurdles (Raye, Mel and Willie Travis) 33.9
- Mel won the pole vault at 11-9
- Won the high jump relay – Mel jumped 5-9

Jeff won its second Hayward Relays title in Eugene in 1959.

- Won long jump relay (Mel, Willie Travis and Dickie Daniels)
- Won 440 relay by beating Medford
- Won the high jump relay – 18 feet, a new record
- Won 880 relay (Ray Hatton, Andrew Clay, Mel and Mike Wyborney)

Jeff won 1959 PIL City Track Meet – Jeff 114 ½ to Grant 108.

- Mel set the 120 high hurdles record in 14.1
- Mel set the 180 low hurdles record in 19.8
- Mel ran the first leg on the 880-yard winning relay

1959 3A Oregon State Track Meet won by South Salem, followed by Beaverton with Jeff third

- Mel won the 180 low hurdles in a state record time of 19.2

- Mel was second to Steve Pauly's national record (13.8) in the 120 high hurdles. He tied the old record at 13.9
- Broke State record in 880-yard relay (Mel, Floyd Wilder, Bob Rattcliff and Raye Renfro) in 1:29.4

Mel's strongest competition at the state track meet during his junior year was Beaverton's Pauly, the defending 1958 champion in both the high and low hurdles.

"Mel was a tough competitor," said Pauly. "Since I trained hard on my form, I was quicker over the high hurdles in 13.8, a 120-yard high hurdles national prep record, but he nipped me in the lows because of his speed."

In 1960, Mel had his third different track coach in three years. Merlin "Bud" White, a former Lewis and Clark track star, came to Jefferson after a year at Wilson and five years at Newport – all coaching track. White was joined by Doug Basham, a Jeff teammate of Mel's oldest bother Dallas and the 1953 PIL double hurdle champion, as the top assistant. The University of Oregon hurdles record-holder when he was in college, Basham worked extensively with Mel in the hurdles.

"I insisted that everyone come to practice and warm up properly," said White. "Mel was very coachable. I would give him a workout schedule and he would follow it. I remember letting him pole vault, but just once. 'That's enough,' I told him afterward, 'you are too valuable if you were to get hurt with an ankle or knee.'"

As Mel continued to improve his technique and speed in his best events, he also ran 100 yards in 9.95 and high jumped 6-2. When he had the opportunity to pole vault, he cleared 12-6 using a steel pole.

His senior 1960 track season became a competitive battle between Jeff and their top rival, Grant.

1960 Hayward Relays – Jeff edged Grant 43-38 to win their third title and retired the trophy.

- Long jump relay (Mel Renfro, Willie Travis and Dickie Daniels) started off with a win
- 440 yard relay (Alvin Bruner, Joe Britt, Andrew Clay and Mike Wyborney) beat Medford
- High jump relay (Wilbur Brown, Ernie Penson and Wyborney) broke the State record of 18 feet
- 880 relay (Ray Hatton, Clay, Renfro and Wyborney) beat Grant
- Jeff's distance medley team took fifth and its shuttle hurdles team took sixth place

1960 PIL City Track Meet – Grant won by ¾ of a point, 79 ½ to Jeff's 78 ¾.

State Track Champions

1960 3A Oregon State Track Meet at Corvallis – Jeff won a lopsided victory with 68 points while Mel scored 32 ½ points.

Renfro Family Collection

Mel scores 32 ½ points with 4 wins and 2 records

- Mel lowered his own 180 low hurdles record 18.9
- Mel set the long jump record .... 24-1 ¼
- Mel won the 110-yard high hurdles 14.0
- Mike Wyborney won the 440 ....49.8
- Larry Jones won the pole vault 12-8
- Jerry Hemstreet was second in the 880 ....1:58.2
- Mel, Clay, Hatton and Wyborney won the 880 Relay...... 1:31.1

Oregon State track coach Sam Bell called Jefferson "the best scoring team in this century."

Golden West Invitational High School Track Athlete of the Year

Mel received an unexpected opportunity to showcase his track talents. He was invited to compete in a national invitational high school meet for the country's top seniors.

Renfro Family collection

Mel honored by *Track and Field News*

The inaugural meet was June 18, 1960, at East Los Angeles City College, sponsored by the Monterey Park Junior Chamber of Commerce. The Portland Junior Chamber of Commerce helped in raising the funds to send Mel and his coaches White and Basham to Los Angeles.

"It was my first time in an airplane," said Mel. "It was one of those prop jobs."

Competing against the cream of the crop of American high school track stars, Mel won the high and low hurdles and finished fourth in the broad jump. Mel just missed the national record in the high hurdles – not once, but twice. He ran 13.8

to win the preliminary heat, then came back to win the final by three yards with the same clocking. Both readings were made against a ten-mile-an-hour wind. National record holder John Truex of North Miami, Florida, finished fifth behind Mel and a trio of Californians.

In the 180-yard lows, Mel won in 19.4 despite running in a headwind. He won easily, with the California champion Bob Bond of Riverside Poly finishing third.

"We, including Mel, were a little miffed when the local papers and wire services failed to mention Renfro as a hurdles contender," said White. "All they could see was Truex and Bond and a couple of other Californians."

Meanwhile, Basham gave the business to a local sportswriter: "R-E-N-F-R-O, that's the way you spell it." Mel passed two jumps in the broad jump and finished with a 22-5 best. Walter Roberts of Compton won with a jump of 23-8, four inches less than Mel's Oregon state record.

"I ran so many heats in the hurdles," remembered Mel, "I didn't have my legs under me to do better in the long jump."

Renfro was voted the outstanding performer in the Golden West Invitational. Mel received the Governor's trophy and was acknowledged as "The 1960 National Track and Field High School Athlete of the Year."

The Golden West Invitational began in 1960 in Los Angeles. The event moved north five years later and was held at various sites around the Sacramento region, including Hughes Stadium, Sacramento State, American River College and Folsom High School. Fifty-three years later, in 2013, the longest running prep classic in the United States moved to the University of California's Edwards Stadium on Berkeley's campus. The roster of GWI champions includes such all-time greats as Jim Ryun, Tommie Smith, Stacy Dragila, Steve Prefontaine, Evelyn Ashford, Rod Milburn, Allyson Felix, Marion Jones, Dwight Stone and Mike Powell. Today, the top two athletes on the national list in each event receive automatic placement in the finals. The top three finalists in each event receive travel compensation.

8

Recruiting

Oregon State coach Tommy Prothro, a top evaluator of football talent, worked hard to recruit Mel Renfro. Prothro enlisted former black player and track star Amos Marsh and freshman Terry Baker to help him. Prothro, who could visualize Mel as a star in his program, was the guest speaker at the Jefferson spring sports banquet. Mel won the school's Hopkin Jenkins trophy as the school's top athlete and was presented a scroll from the Wigwam Wiseman, recognizing him as a high school football All-American.

Meanwhile, Mel became a recruiting enigma to University of Oregon coach Len Casanova. The man who was a father-figure image to so many of his football players found Mel to be rather quiet and unresponsive to his initial recruiting tactics.

"He was the funniest kid I ever recruited," recalled Casanova. "I couldn't connect with him. He was too shy to declare himself, but his dad said, 'Keep trying, I think you are doing all right.'"

But the coach was aware that Mel's former teammate, Baker – the quarterback with whom he had shared two state championship seasons at Jefferson – was returning to football at Oregon State. It was obvious that Mel would be interested in joining him to be part of another winning combination.

Casanova resorted to his best instincts and decided on a different strategy by recruiting Mel's parents, Dallas and Edna. It was apparent that they had an increased interest since their son Raye's recruitment had collapsed the year before. Casanova also enlisted the company of Oregon track coach Bill Bowerman to sit down with the parents and paint a picture of success for arguably the nation's best two-sport high school recruit.

Bowerman knew what he was doing when he joined Casanova in the process to get Mel to the Eugene campus. Mel could be part of the plan for his challenge for the 1962 NCAA track championships, the event the track coach worked hard to land in Eugene. The team's reputation was already gaining momentum as a distance-team powerhouse. To add the nation's top track and field high school athlete of 1960 with strengths in the hurdles, sprints, and long jump would be a huge addition to his dream.

It worked. The Oregon coaches convinced the parents they would both look after Mel's best interests, academically, socially and athletically.

Mel, with the intention of entering Oregon State in a few weeks, was stunned when his father broke the news to him: "Melvin, you are going to Oregon." Obedient and respectful to his parent's wishes, Mel obeyed and matriculated at the University of Oregon.

Mel was not aware of any enticements that summer, but in a 2015 interview he admitted, "I didn't pay any attention to it at the time, but Dad did get a nice 1957 Chevrolet that fall, a car he drove for years."

The Shrine Game

With Mel's declaration he was going to Oregon behind him, he turned to the two-week preparation for the Shrine Game, which pitted the Metro All-Stars against the State All-Star team. Jefferson's Tom DeSylvia was selected as the head coach while Jeff teammates Herb Washburn, Ken Kearney and Mike Barnes joined Mel.

The Oregon high school all-star football game has always been a showcase for the future college players. The Shrine Game's history goes back to its first game in 1948, which became a coming-out-game for a certain Sam Baker (no relation to Terry) from Corvallis High School. His booming punts, long runs and interception earned him the MVP award. Baker, who later starred at Oregon State, had a 15-year NFL career as a kicker and fullback with three different teams. His antics and comical behavior during his time in Dallas became Cowboy lore. Baker, the punter and kicker, was always testing team rules and the patience of their third-year coach, Tom Landry. "Baker was born to be an irritant to me," he complained. After two seasons, Baker was traded. The expansion team struggled until it drafted good young players and became a competitive NFL team.

Reported the *Portland Reporter:* "Marvelous Mel Renfro, the versatile athlete from Jefferson, led the Metros to victory 27-13, as expected. He scored the game's first touchdown in the second quarter to place his mates in front, and netted 113 yards on nine plays for a rousing 12.5 average. For his performance, Mel received the Most Valuable Player Award, following in the footsteps of Terry Baker, who won the honor last year."

Renfro family collection

Shrine All-Star game MVP

Lee Gustafson, the South Salem coach, commented on Mel before the Shrine All-Star Game in 1960: "Renfro could have made many college teams in the country last year. Watch the way he changes pace. He looks like he's going full speed, then half speed and then all of a sudden – zoom."

DeSylvia declared emphatically, **"Mel's the best all-around football player I've ever coached or seen."**

College and Frosh Football

Mel recalled that Warren Robinson, a man who owned a neighborhood grocery store, volunteered to transport him down to Eugene. Mel's first away-from-home experience was living in the "jock dormitory" across from Hayward Field. He enrolled as a physical education major and roomed with another freshman, football teammate Montee Fitchet. Two other black players, Ron Stratton and Lu Bain, joined Mel on the 41-member freshman football team, which also included Mike Helfrich, a tackle on that team and the father of Oregon's present head coach Mark.

In his early days at Oregon, Mel was undemonstrative and restrained in his new environment. "He was shy, but never sullen," said a friend. "But Mel always had those friendly eyes. He just didn't say much."

That was confirmed on a weekend trip with college friends to San Francisco, also a new experience. Mel was ribbed for saying only three words. "That was me," he said.

A 99-percent white community, Eugene welcomed its black student-athletes with open arms, especially if they could perform adequately on the field. Mel was received warmly and was treated well with great respect.

"The chancellor of the school invited me to his house for a party," said Mel. "It may have been unusual, but it was just great and I enjoyed that welcome atmosphere."

Meanwhile, Bob Berry, a star quarterback from San Jose, was closing his recruitment when assistant coach John Robinson encouraged him: "Bob, you've got to come up to Oregon; we just got the best running back in the country." Berry had just played in an All-Star Game with some pretty good players and felt Robinson was probably stretching the truth. But on his arrival to Oregon, Berry was blown away with the athletic and football talent of Mel Renfro: "I hadn't seen anyone like him." The two freshmen football prospects would complement each other. Both future All-Americans?

Frosh football was limited to only five weeks of practice, with four games against other freshman teams. The rule was changed later to allow freshmen to play varsity, but at the time it seemed a good transition-to-college time for first-year players. Robinson, of future USC and Los Angeles Rams fame, was selected to coach his first team. The talented 1960 Oregon frosh team handily won all four games.

Robby was really a good coach," recalled Mel. "He was very funny. The guy had a speech impediment. He stuttered terribly. But he was easy to get along with and was well-liked by all the players."

John Robinson and his Daly City, California, friend, future Pro Football Hall of Famer John Madden, had come to Oregon in 1954. Although Madden didn't stick around after the freshman season, Robinson remained. During his senior year, he had limited time as an end on Oregon's 1958 Rose Bowl team, but his football smarts were recognized. He was hired by Casanova as an assistant coach. "Robby" was an Oregon assistant for 10 years for both Casanova and Jerry Frei. He served as an offensive coordinator at USC in 1972 for John McKay, who was an Oregon assistant when Robinson played there. After a stint with Madden and the Oakland Raiders, Robinson coached USC from 1976 to 1982 and 1993 to 1997, posting a 104-35-4 record, five conference championships and seven of eight bowl victories, including four Rose Bowls. He coached the Los Angeles Rams from 1983 to 1991 with a 79-74 record and two NFC title games. He was elected to the College Football Hall of Fame in 2009.

Robinson, interviewed in March 2011, had this to say: "The 1960 Oregon Frosh was my first team to coach. It was a good recruiting class of strong people, and just good football people."

Robinson had the highest praise for Mel: "I can remember going up to Washington to play the 'Pups.' We were forced to play on their practice field down by the lake due to the rain. Washington had almost 70 players on the sidelines compared to the 25 to 30 we had. Renfro scored three back-to-back touchdowns. It was almost funny. We just killed them, 62-12."

"Mel was such a good college football player. He made a phenomenal impact. If we had used him as an I-formation tailback, as we did later with the tailbacks I had when I was at USC, he may have won the Heisman Trophy. **Mel was as good a player as I've coached and would rank him up there with Marcus Allen and Eric Dickerson."**

9

Varsity Football

Mel often suffered night restlessness and pre-game anxiety throughout his college career.

"I get very nervous and I didn't want to show it," he admitted. "Along about Friday, the food starts to taste bad. When I try to eat on the day of a game, I just put it down, even though I knew it wasn't good for me."

Before his first collegiate game against Idaho in 1961, Mel went through some 48 hours of his pre-game agony.

"Mel Renfro proved himself human right from the start," wrote the *Oregonian*'s John White. "The first time he ever carried the ball for the University of Oregon, he gained only three yards. But the next time he touched the ball he went 80 yards to a touchdown."

Mel had a great game. He carried the ball from scrimmage only four times, but gained 122 yards. He returned one punt 42 yards and caught another pass for 20 yards while playing only 15 minutes in the 51-0 rout of the Vandals.

1961	**(4-6)**		
S23	Idaho	W	51-0
S30	@ Utah	L	6-14
O7	@Minnesota	L	7-14
O14	Arizona	L	6-15
O21	San Jose State	W	21-6
O28	Washington	W	7-6
N4	@Stanford	W	19-7
N11	@Washington State	L	21-22
N18	@Ohio State	L	12-22
N25	Oregon State	L	2-6

Even though Mel got off to an impressive start, for the first time in his football career he had to deal with an injury. He got hurt early in the Utah game, which the Ducks lost 14-6.

"I chipped a bone in my right ankle," said Mel. "After our trainer, Bob 'Two Gun' Officer, taped it, I went back into the game for a couple of plays, but it wouldn't go. I had what I called 'sprinter's ankles.' They were too delicate."

Mel missed the next four games of his sophomore year, during which Oregon lost at Minnesota 14-7, lost to Arizona 15-6, beat San Jose State 21-6 and squeezed past Washington 7-6. Mel returned to action for the Stanford game, despite the fact he was still hurting.

Mel's limited playing time at Stanford became his best offensive performance as a sophomore. It was extraordinary. Oregon offensive coach Max Coley had alerted *The Oregon Journal* sportswriter George Pasero, saying that if the right time came, he would call on Renfro.

"Well, it did – not far from the Stanford goal," recalled Pasero in a 1996 interview. "Renfro touched the ball just five times and was responsible for three touchdowns. He ran four yards for one touchdown, returned a kickoff 94 yards for a second and threw a 39-yard scoring pass to Paul Burleson for a third." Oregon won 19-7. "That was Red Grange stuff," recalled Pasero. **"Mel Renfro was the best all-around back I've seen at Oregon."**

After the Ducks lost a close game to Washington State 22-21, they faced a huge physical challenge playing the Big Ten's Ohio State in Columbus. The Buckeyes dressed 119 scholarship players, were undefeated and featured a strong runner in senior fullback Bob Ferguson in their "Five yards and a cloud of dust" offense to go with a budding sophomore sensation named Paul Warfield.

Mel gained national recognition with his offensive and superb defensive play.

"When we played the Buckeyes, they were supposed to run all over us," said Mel. "Yet they only beat us 22-12. When I would see their All-American Bob Ferguson coming, I came up and met him head-on-head – many times." Mel, from his safety position, performed like an extra linebacker making 25 tackles, 15 unassisted. Ohio State coach Woody Hayes became upset. "He was livid on the sidelines," said Mel. "And even after the game, Hayes was still screaming and hollering at his team."

Ohio State remained undefeated by clobbering Michigan the following week 50-20, earning them the Big 10 title and the No. 2 ranking in the nation behind Alabama. Ferguson was runner-up for the Heisman. But oddly, the Buckeye faculty refused a Rose Bowl bid.

The Civil War

Mel often referred to his Civil War games with rival Oregon State as his "Achilles' heel." He personally took the blame for Oregon's season-ending 6-2 loss in 1961 due to two second-half plays – the first a fourth-down run, and then an intercepted halfback pass.

Just 24 hours before the kickoff of the Civil War game, the grass turf at Hayward Field was buried under a three-inch blanket of snow. The field was cleared by game time and the only evidence was the banks of snow on the sidelines. The playing surface was soggy, but playable.

The Oregon State victory was a physical "slug-fest." For the most part, it was a defensive battle between Oregon's defense stopping junior quarterback Terry Baker and for the Beavers' defense holding the Ducks' sophomore Mel Renfro in check.

The game became a series of errors, fumbles and interceptions from the start. In the first quarter, Baker faded back on the Oregon 26, then started to run before spotting Herb Washburn, the former Jefferson All-State end, in the end zone for an apparent touchdown. However the officials abolished the score claiming Baker was past the line of scrimmage when he threw the ball. The ensuing penalty added to the Beaver drive stalling at the Oregon 31.

Halfway through the second period, Oregon State's Gene Hilliard intercepted a Renfro halfback pass at the 50, but it led only to a missed Beaver field goal from the 15. A reversal of fortune for Oregon followed, by fumbling a pitchout allowing Beaver Roger Johnson to recover the ball on the Oregon 16. In two plays, Tom Gates scored the game's only touchdown.

During the third period Oregon scored a two-point safety, when the Beavers, backed up against their own goal line, hiked the ball over the punter's head and out of the end zone...making the score 6-2.

But the turning point of the game came in the middle of the third quarter when Mel Renfro was stopped on downs on the one-yard line after Oregon moved 70 yards on the game's longest drive. On first down Mel was thrown for a three-yard loss back to the five-yard line. On the fourth attempt, big Neil Plumley blocked Mel's path while Ross Cariago filled the gap hitting Mel in mid-air, short of the goal line. The Sunday *Oregonian* banner read: ***Oregon's Prize Plum Plucked in Mid-Air*** above an end zone photograph of the play.

With 2:29 left, Oregon had a drive going reaching the Beaver 37 when Oregon State halfback Bill Monk picked off another Mel Renfro halfback pass on the 30, ending Oregon's final opportunity to win.

For Mel's first Civil War, he carried most of the Oregon offense by netting 67 tough yards running and caught one pass for 7 yards while throwing two interceptions. On defense, he was in on many tackles and intercepted a Baker pass. Mel gave his perception of the game: "The weather was cold and snowy," said Mel. "It was a hard-hitting defensive affair for both teams. Late in the game, we had the ball on the two-yard line, and if we score, we win. They gave it to me on a sweep. Of course everyone in the stadium knew I was going to get the ball, so the Beavers stacked that side and I didn't make it. There was nothing there and Oregon State won. Afterward, I felt like a piece of broken glass. I had played so hard and got beat up so bad."

Football Health

Before the Civil War game, the ankle injury had hampered Mel and his team's productivity for six games, keeping him out of four games against Minnesota, Arizona, San Jose State and Washington, while limiting him to just a few plays in the Utah and Stanford games. Mel's value to the team was reflected in the stats. He still led the team in rushing with 335 yards on just 61 carries and tied with running back Lu Bain in scoring with a mere 24 points. The 1961 Oregon team finished 4-6. A healthy Mel would have made a huge difference, both offensively and defensively. He needed to stay healthy.

"Playing both ways was a challenge. I probably would have set more records and done a lot more offensively had I stuck to offense," said Mel. "I was on the field all the time – offense, defense and special teams. I played hard every play. You make a stop on defense, then you field a punt and run it up a ways, and then you're on offense running the ball. That can wear you out. They would platoon us in and out, but you couldn't always give your best, although you wanted to. Your body wouldn't allow it."

Disappointed with his sophomore football season, Mel eagerly focused on his next challenge, college track. If he could regain his health and speed, he could enjoy football again.

10

NCAA Track Champions

In the spring, Mel would walk from the football practice field to Hayward Field for track practice. As a two-sport athlete, he had a busy schedule. In 1962, Mel was up to it, and it became an All-American year for him in two major sports. It was arguably the finest year ever for an Oregon athlete.

It would also be a track season in which Oregon's legendary coach and co-founder of Nike, Bill Bowerman, would prove himself as one of the best in the business.

"Bowerman gave us a tremendous workout schedule to get us in shape for track," said Mel. "We were always running the golf course and doing very difficult exercises – the toughest I had ever done. Bill just laid it on us. We would run 220s with a baton handing off six to eight times in a row. As a goal, I got so I could jog the curves while sprinting the straight-away to complete a mile, all under a five-minute limit."

Bowerman finally had the stable of athletes to accomplish the goals he could only dream about before – an upset dual-meet win, two world relay records and the NCAA team championship.

Kenny Moore in his biography, *Bowerman and the Men of Oregon*, was able to document the events:

USC Dual Meet Upset

The first major accomplishment came with challenging mighty USC in a dual meet in the LA Coliseum. The Trojans had not lost a dual meet since 1945, racking up 129 straight victories. Bowerman, a wizard in strategizing and placing track athletes in different events to maximize the scoring, was up to the challenge.

The scoring for a dual meet was on a 5-3-1 basis. Oregon won nine of the 15 events and tied for first in another, upsetting the favored Trojans 75-56 for their first dual-meet loss in 17 years.

- Dyrol Burleson, Archie San Romani and steeplechaser Clayton Steinke swept the mile for nine points.
- Sophomore Les Tipton threw 20 feet further than his personal best in the javelin to upset world-ranked Jan Sikorski with a throw of 238-4. John Burns got third to give the Ducks six points in the event.
- Jerry Close won the broad jump with Mel Renfro second for eight points in the event.
- Burleson, San Romani and a fresh Sig Ohlemann swept the half-mile for another nine points.
- Vic Reeve, Keith Forman, and Mike Lehner swept the two mile. Another nine points.
- Jerry Tarr won both hurdles for 10 points.
- Harry Jerome won both sprints for 10 points.

West Coast Relays

While most of Oregon's track squad went to Seattle for a dual meet with Washington, Bowerman found the opportunity to send his talented four-mile relay team to the West Coast Relays in Fresno, California, in an effort to define the progress of his distance runners. Western Michigan was the only competition in the event, so each miler ran against the clock.

Mel was in Seattle with the track team while the Oregon football team was playing its annual game with the Alumni. He was only partially excused from spring football practice.

At the Relays, San Romani led off with a 4:03.5 mile. He was followed by Reeve's 4:05.2. Forman ran a 4:02.5 mile before handing off to Burleson, who ran the anchor mile in 3:57.7. Oregon's accumulative time was 16:08.9, beating New Zealand's world record by 14.9 seconds.

440-Yard Relay World Record Tied

On May 26, 1962, Mel teamed up with fellow football players Jerry Tarr and Mike Gaechter and the Canadian star Harry Jerome at the California Relays in Modesto, California, to win the 440-yard relay in 40 seconds flat and tie the world record.

Jeff Eberhart of Oregon's sports department recapped the event: "Renfro opened the race for Oregon, handing off to Gaechter for the second leg. At this point, Oregon was trailing the Los Angeles Striders and Texas Southern. Gaechter injured his hamstring just before handing the baton to Tarr, but made the handoff, and Tarr took off, closing the distance on the opponents to one half-stride. With the transfer of the baton to the anchor man, Jerome just exploded, taking the lead with 40 yards and winning by two feet over the Striders' anchor. Oregon had tied the world record, and according to Tarr would have set a new world record if he hadn't waited for Gaechter's handoff."

Jerome also had a second big win that day. He won the 100-yard dash in a meet record 9.3 seconds, beating Florida A&M's Bob Hayes, who was previously unbeaten. In Hayes' 62-race career, he was beaten only twice.

Hayes would break the 100-meter world record at the 1964 Summer Olympics in Tokyo. He followed that with a second gold medal in the 4x100-meter relay. His come-from-behind win for the U.S. team in the relay became one of the most memorable of Olympic moments while producing a new world record. Coincidentally, within two years, Mel and Bob Hayes would become teammates in professional football.

1962 NCAA Track Championship

Bowerman, who chaired the NCAA rules committee, campaigned to host the nationals in Eugene. Oregon was awarded the 1962 National Collegiate Championships at Hayward Field after he convinced Athletic Director Leo Harris to widen the track to eight lanes. It was a step forward in making Eugene, Oregon, "The Track Capital of America."

The scoring for the top six places was on a 10-8-6-4-2-1 basis. Oregon won the NCAA Championship with 85 points, more than the next three teams combined.

- Jerome placed second in the 100 to Villanova's Frank Budd's 9.4, then came back to win the 220 for 18 points.
- Burleson won his third straight NCAA mile in 3:59.8, with Forman fourth for 14 points.
- Tarr won the 120 high hurdles in 13.5 and the 440 low hurdles in 50.3 for 20 points.
- Renfro placed third behind Oklahoma's Anthony Watson and Ohio State's Paul Warfield in the broad jump, then placed second to Tarr in the 120 highs for 14 points.

- Dave Steen placed fifth in the shot put; Lehner and Steinke were third and fourth in the steeplechase; Tipton took fifth in the javelin; Terry Llewellyn tied for second in the high jump. Combined, that provided Oregon with 21 points.

Mel credits weight loss and Bowerman's coaching for his success in the broad jump. In Friday's qualifying, Mel placed second at 25-11, an Oregon record, while scratching at 26-8. During Saturday's finals, Mel scratched three jumps over 26 feet, yet still placed third with Friday's qualifying distance.

In the 120 high hurdles, Mel ran 14.0 in the qualifying heat, placing second while hitting the seventh and eighth hurdles. Tarr took first place in the hurdles finals on Saturday in 13.5. However, Mel had been leading the race at the halfway mark and might have won had he not hit the final hurdle. Mel would finish in a time of 13.8 seconds, finishing second.

"I could see Tarr out of the corner of my left eye," recalled Mel. "He was coming hard...I could never beat him."

Kenny Moore captured the spirit of the moment in the biography *Bowerman and the Men of Oregon*:

"Bowerman seemed to be everywhere, at his beatific best, calming, congratulating, in full command. The next day, however, he had trouble controlling his emotion when he opened the Eugene *Register Guard*. There was a photo of Renfro and Tarr midway through the highs, 'both looking just the way they were taught,' Bowerman said. 'Peering out under their eyebrows.'" (A Bowerman discipline for head position while training hurdlers.)

NCAA Track All-American

Nine Oregon track stars were named All-American based on their efforts at the championships: Harry Jerome, Dyrol Burleson, Jerry Tarr, Mel Renfro, Mike Lehner, Keith Forman, Dave Steen and Les Tipton.

Mel described Coach Bowerman as a workaholic.

"He had us doing some incredible things, just running, running, running, all the time," Renfro said. "There's no mystery to why he had such successful athletes, and had so many records and championships. He did so many innovative things. He was always a step ahead of everyone else. It was a joy performing for him."

In turn, Bowerman had tremendous admiration for Mel Renfro's contribution in 1962. The coach described him as **"a great football player and athlete, one of the best to go through this institution."**

"One day during the winter my sophomore year when I was inside the indoor field house, I was trying out a bamboo pole for the very first time," said Mel. "Although I cleared 13 feet in high school with a steel pole, it was like nothing when I cleared 15 feet. But, as I was moving the bar higher, I got the word."

Renfro collection

1962 Track All-American

"Renfro, put that pole down!" screamed Bowerman. "I never want to see that pole in your hands again."

For perspective: Marty Frank, Oregon's top pole-vaulter, had a personal best of 14-8.

Bill Bowerman was the University of Oregon head track coach for 24 seasons, from July of 1948 to 1972. Over his career, he trained 31 Olympic athletes, 51 All-Americans, 12 American record-holders, 24 NCAA champions and 16 sub-4-minute milers. His teams won four NCAA titles and finished in the top 10 in the nation 16 times. He coached the first "high-altitude" training program for the 1968 Mexico City Olympics, which led to his selection as the head track coach for the 1972 Munich Olympics. In the 1960s, he introduced the New Zealand concept of jogging to the United States with his three-page guide, which ignited the jogging phenomenon. In 1964, he co-founded Blue Ribbon Sports, an athletic footwear distribution company later known as Nike, with Phil Knight. He helped design the "Nike Cortez," a top seller, ruining his wife's waffle iron. Bowerman's legacy extends to the National Distance Hall of Fame, the USA National Track and Field Hall of Fame, the Oregon Sports Hall of Fame and Oregon's Athletic Hall of Fame. His statue holding a stopwatch graces the northwest corner of Hayward Field, and the Nike Headquarters is located on Bowerman Drive in Beaverton, Oregon.

Mel didn't compete in the postseason AAU track meets. He was going to marry Pat Burch in July. The couple had a four-year relationship extending back to high school at Jefferson.

Pat met the Renfro family at church when she was 12 years old. "At that time I only knew Melvin's parents, Dallas and Edna, and his older brother James and his fiancée Vilma," recalled Pat. "I didn't meet Melvin until he was a junior at Jefferson."

"Despite being from the same neighborhood and attending the same church for a while," said Mel, "I didn't notice Pat until she was a freshman. Socially in high school, guys always went together to functions and dances while the girls did the same. When I took an interest in her we would go to the parks and little parties together. In the meantime, I got to know her folks and little brothers, Sonny and Micheal, well. Later when our relationship got serious, we decided to play a waiting game. We would wait until Pat graduated from high school to get married."

The track experience was excellent preparation for Mel's junior football season. His conditioning and added speed allowed him to stay healthy and perform well.

"The high hurdles really helped me for football," said Mel. "It was developing the expertise to come out of the blocks to the first hurdle that developed my quickness for football. That explosion off the line with the high knees would help my game."

Oregon's tough football schedule on the national stage would expose his talents for the many honors that would come his way.

11

Consensus All-American

MEL AND CLARE "PAT" BURCH WERE MARRIED ON JULY 14, 1962, AT Hughes Memorial Methodist Church in North Portland, the replanted church the Renfro family helped establish from the city of Vanport.

The newlyweds made an easy transition to the campus at the University of Oregon.

"The first couple of months after our marriage," said Pat, "We lived in Portland until it was time for Melvin to begin football practice. Then we moved to Eugene to live in married student housing. The first year when Melvin attended classes, football and track practice, I attended classes myself and worked in the Chancellor's office. In the fall of 1962, I was elected by the student body to be the hostess for Dads Day Weekend. I considered that quite an honor."

For Mel, the success of Oregon's track team as NCAA champion and his personal recognition as an All-American in track and field weren't fully realized at the time. His primary focus was to get in good shape and stay healthy in an effort to avoid another frustrating football season. Before 1961, Mel had always been healthy, and losing football games wasn't acceptable.

Oregon began the 1962 season with optimism. Coach Len Casanova figured this would be his most talented team since he'd been at the school, but he shuddered when he scoured the schedule, the likes of Texas, Rice, Air Force, Ohio State and Oregon State.

Mel was in top shape and sophomore quarterback Bob Berry was back after a year away. Berry showcased his talent during spring practice. He had the passing skills, the poise and the toughness to balance the running attack. Joining Berry and Mel in the backfield were juniors Larry Hill and Lu Bain. The quartet became known as "The Firehouse Four," a tag given them by sports information director Hal Childs.

The linemen, tagged "The Baby Bulls" by trainer Bob Officer, would be tackles Ron Snidow and Steve Barnett, and guards Mickey Ording and Dennis Prozinski, Mel's high school teammate. They were joined by tough end Dave Wilcox, a transfer from Boise JC who also became a major player.

Breakup of the Pacific Coast Conference

During Mel's college career, Oregon played as an independent. Scheduling became a huge problem. Instead of playing USC, UCLA, and California, the Ducks were forced to accept away games with Minnesota, Ohio State, Texas, Rice, Air Force and West Virginia. Only Indiana, Utah, Penn State, Arizona and San Jose State would visit Eugene or Portland.

The breakup of the Pacific Coast Conference came in 1958 after conference officials suspended USC and UCLA for alleged recruiting violations. The guilty schools balked and complained to the California Regents before withdrawing from the PCC. That was followed by the exodus of the rest of the California schools.

Hendrik Van Leuven in his book, *Touchdown UCLA,* published in 1982, detailed the conference breakup: "Slush funds, money covertly provided by alums and booster groups, took place in varying degrees at every school, were tacitly accepted by the entire conference, and as long as everyone kept their mouths shut, no one would get hurt. The slush funds were against PCC rules, referred to as the 'Purity Code,' written by Orlando Hollis, dean of law at Oregon and a dominant voice in the PCC for years. It was just a matter of time before the hypocrisy of the conference-wide situation was exposed. The slush funds at UCLA and USC were exposed first. Then after John Cherberg, head coach at Washington, was fired in 1956, he blew the whistle on a Husky slush-fund in retaliation.

"Both California and Stanford revealed different levels of violations. The penalties were not accepted well. UCLA coach Red Sanders' fight against the PCC was dramatically effective in bringing about its self-destruction. The California Board of Regents and the Board of Trustees for USC withdrew from the conference."

The next year, five of the schools, Washington, UCLA, Stanford, California and USC, formed the Athletic Association of Western Universities (AAWU), also known as the Big-5 Conference. Washington State came back into the fold in 1962 to form the Big-6. It wasn't until the 1964 season that Oregon and Oregon State were invited to join the conference. Left out from the old PCC was Idaho. In 1968 the conference was called the Pacific-Eight or the PAC-8.

1962	**(6-3-1)**		
S22	@Texas	L	13-25
S29	Utah	W	35-8
O6	San Jose State	W	14-0
O13	@Rice	W	31-12
O20	@Air Force	W	35-20
O27	@Washington	T	21-21
N3	Stanford	W	28-14
N10	Washington State	W	28-10
N17	@Ohio State	L	7-26
N24	@Oregon State	L	17-20

Texas

Oregon flew into Austin for the opener against Texas, one of the nation's top teams. Anticipating Southern segregation policies at the hotel, Casanova took the lead so racial issues wouldn't bother his black players. "Cas told the hotel in no uncertain terms," remembered Bob Berry, "serve us all or we will cancel the game and fly home."

Oregon opened the evening game with a strong showing. The Ducks' speed dominated the Longhorns in the first half and they led 13-3, while holding the hosts to two first downs and 71 yards. On Larry Hill's very first carry as a starter, he ran off tackle for 30 yards and a touchdown. It wasn't until six minutes lapsed in the third quarter before the Longhorns' third-string line sparked a comeback.

"We had them on the ropes," said Mel. "We had them beat before we fumbled a handoff and they recovered inside the ten. That gave them an easy touchdown."

The Longhorns hit quickly for 22 points in 12 minutes and defeated Oregon 25-13. Mel remembers his team wilting from the heat.

"We just weren't prepared for the Texas heat," he said. "We ran Texas ragged for two and a half quarters, and then the 90-degree heat got to us."

Renfro's running made a big impression on Texas coach Darrell Royal. "We've never been up against a back with his speed, balance and finesse," Royal said. "He must have had more than two legs. Anyone with only two legs couldn't get around like he does."

Motivated by their strong early showing and subsequent disappointment in losing, the Ducks hoped for a postseason bowl rematch. Co-captain Steve Barnett stated he wanted his team to be in the Cotton Bowl on New Year's Day for a return engagement against a Texas team he and his teammates felt they should have beaten.

Following a home 35-8 victory over Utah, in which Mel played well, gaining 120 yards on just eight carries, and a 14-0 shutout of San Jose State, Oregon returned to Texas to play Rice in Houston.

Segregation in Southern College Football

In the South, all-white teams were the norm into the late 1960s as the region was slow to embrace civil rights, especially in something as cherished as college football. The University of Texas admitted black students in 1956, but did not lift the ban on them playing varsity sports until 1963. Even then, Coach Darrell Royal acknowledged, there was tacit pressure from university regents for him not to rush to integrate the football team.

When Texas beat Arkansas 15-14 in Fayetteville in what was billed as the Game of the Century, President Richard Nixon declared the Longhorns the national champions. The 1969 Longhorns were the last all-white team to win a national college football championship. That was to change. Their first recruited black player was Julius Whittier, but as a freshman, he wasn't eligible to play.

Alabama of the SEC also changed its stance about desegregating its football team in 1970. The Crimson Tide were unable to play a number of teams from the North because many of those schools did not want to play a team entrenched in segregation. So Coach Bear Bryant looked out West, and USC agreed to travel into the Deep South for a matchup of two of the best programs in the nation. Alabama players and fans were surprised to see the number of black players on USC's roster. USC had an all-black backfield. The Trojans' star running back, Sam Cunningham, ran over and through the Alabama defenders as the all-white crowd at the game could only sit back in shock, watching what black athletes were capable of doing. USC won 42-21. In a roundabout way, Cunningham ended segregation on Alabama's football team. The very next year, the Crimson Tide had a black player on their roster, and now 40 years later, nearly all their team is black.

Rice

The Rice game presented Mel Renfro with "the first and only time I had to address racial discrimination during my college career," he said.

The Friday night before the game, the Ducks searched 17 movie theaters before they found one that would allow black players. The entire Oregon football team attended in solidarity while sitting in the balcony.

Since Mel hailed from Houston as a child, he considered the game a personal homecoming. Most of segregated Rice Stadium was off-limits to African-Americans, but at Mel's request, an exception was made. An area was roped off on the 35-yard line for his grandfather, aunts, uncles and cousins to see him play. "It was the first time as a young adult that I was able to see my grandfather," remembered Mel. "I got to wave at him when I left the field. For me, it was really a very touching moment."

Renfro responded with one of his finest football games. Mel played his heart out. As 30,000 watched, he flew past tacklers 13 times for 141 yards, scored himself on the first drive, set up another with runs of 40 and 20 yards, caught two passes for 27 yards and returned an intercepted pass 65 yards to set up another touchdown. He had 233 all-purpose yards in a stunning 32-12 victory. It was Oregon's first triumph over a team from Texas. "It was amazing," said Casanova. "The Rice fans gave Mel a standing ovation, and in those days, for a black athlete – that was something."

Jess Neely, the 23rd-year coach at Rice who had seen his Owls play many of the top football teams in the nation, was quoted following the game: "I couldn't remember seeing a better back than Renfro was out there, and I think Oregon has more speed than any team we've ever played. In fact, I know they have."

"The Houston press was equally generous with Oregon and Renfro," wrote the *Register Guard's* Dick Strite. "They were impressed with the overall team speed and Renfro's prowess as one of the great college football players of all time." A Houston headline pronounced alliteratively, "Renfro Runs Rice Ragged."

"God blessed me to have a good game," said Mel. "It made an

impression on the fans and my kin folks. They talked for years about the day little Melvin came down to Houston and did all these things and got us in the game.' Mel considered the Rice game **"the highlight of his college football career."**

Air Force

The following week took the upbeat Duck football team to meet the tough Ben Martin–coached Air Force Academy. Oregon dampened the dedication of new 52,000-seat Falcon Stadium by winning 35-20.

Although Air Force slowed down Mel's offensive running game, he still excelled. On Larry Hill's 50-yard TD run, Mel threw two blocks on the same play to free him.

"Tremendous second effort," said Casanova. On defense, Mel slowed running quarterback Terry Isaacson with such a hard hit, it caused him to cartwheel backward. The Falcons' star didn't figure in any big gain after that, while Oregon outgained them 489 to 297 yards.

Washington

Week six's game, played in Seattle against undefeated Washington, was another hard-hitting battle. The *Oregonian*'s sports page pictured a Renfro-signature hurdle when he scored in the first quarter. Washington answered with an extraordinary rushing game, running from the huddle and smashing for first downs without any passes, scoring on a Charlie Mitchell run to tie the game. Mel answered the second Husky rushing TD in the third quarter with a 14-yard halfback pass to Greg Willener, but the Ducks missed the extra point. After Washington scored again following a blocked punt, the Ducks took to the air, only to have two long drives stopped.

With time running out, and Oregon down eight points, Mel made an outstanding play. He went back attempting a desperation pass and was forced to run. He reversed field and eluded tacklers for a 47-yard gain to the Husky 18. It became the game's turning point. On the next play, Hill busted the last 18 yards for the countering touchdown. A Berry bootleg pass to Dick Imwalle for the two-point conversion tied the game. The game ended that way. The 21-21 tie was the fifth in the long Oregon-Washington rivalry.

Even after a 26-7 loss at Ohio State, the Ducks were 6-2-1, and had been contacted by Bluebonnet Bowl officials about a bid for the postseason game in Texas. It would be offered if the Ducks defeated Oregon State in the Civil War game. Casanova had decided not to tell his team before the game.

Civil War

Berry ran for a touchdown, then later found Mel breaking past the Beaver pass defenders and lofted a 50-yard pass to him for a touchdown. The Ducks led 17-6 at halftime, and Casanova wanted to make sure there wasn't a letdown. The coach relented and told his team about the bowl bid.

Oregon State, with quarterback Terry Baker, marched the Beavers to a touchdown on the opening drive of the second half. Later, Baker had them threatening again at the Oregon 18 before Wilcox threw him for losses on two consecutive plays. On fourth down at the 34-yard line, OSU's Rich Brooks, the future Oregon coach, lofted a "pooch" punt to the 15-yard line, and the ball took a weird bounce and hit Mel's leg. The Beavers recovered. On fourth down, Oregon State resorted to a pre-planned play to catch Mel off guard.

Mel's former high school teammate, the left-handed Baker, rolled out to his right to run or pass. When Mel rotated to the sideline in anticipation, Baker stopped, faked right, and then threw a pass crossfield to Danny Espalin, who had curled out of the backfield up the center, for an easy 13-yard touchdown. Oregon State won 20-17. Baker, who was to win the Heisman Trophy that season, was carried off the field by his teammates and Oregon State was invited to the Liberty Bowl.

"The blame for the Oregon State loss was squarely on my shoulders," Mel recalled. "That was very disappointing. That has stayed with me."

The team, which Casanova called his best while at Oregon, wasn't invited to a bowl game. But the Ducks gained a school-record 3,530 yards of total offense. Mel set school single-season records in rushing (783 yards), touchdowns (13) and points (78).

Honors

Because of the national scheduling, Oregon's Mel Renfro gained the necessary exposure to become a consensus All-American, thus overcoming an "East coast media bias" that often eliminated proper recognition for players in the West.

An example of that media bias was Oregon's superb quarterback George Shaw playing in the Pacific Coast Conference his 1954 senior season. He suffered from lack of national exposure despite leading the nation in total offense with 1,536 yards. *Sports Illustrated* called him "Six-way Shaw." He passed, ran, caught passes, punted, kicked off, and kicked extra points besides calling the plays and playing defense as a safety. Shaw became the Baltimore Colts "bonus" pick as the NFL's No. 1 draft pick, but was not selected for any All-American first teams. Shaw also split the West Coast votes with California's quarterback Paul Larson, allowing Notre Dame's Ralph Guglielmi to gain consensus first-team recognition at QB.

Honors came in for Mel. He became a consensus All-American along with his Jefferson High teammate, Oregon State's Baker, an extraordinary achievement for a couple of Oregonians. Mel earned first-team recognition from the United Press International, Walter

Camp Football Foundation, the *Sporting News*, and *Time Magazine*. Individually, Mel won the Pigskin Club of Washington DC Trophy as the outstanding collegiate back in the nation. Baker won almost everything else.

Terry Baker became the most decorated college football player of all time and the first Heisman winner west of Texas. The Academic All-American also won the Maxwell, the Helms, the Voit, the Pop Warner, the Hayward, and a plaque presented to him by Len Casanova as the outstanding athlete to compete against his Ducks. When *Sports Illustrated* honored Baker as its 1962 Sportsman of the Year, he became the only college footballer to be so honored, even to this day. The Los Angeles Rams' scouting report gave Baker its highest rating as a pro prospect.

Baker was the No. 1 pick in the 1963 draft. But the honors didn't translate into success for Baker in pro football. The Rams' situation was not a good fit for him. After three seasons in the NFL and another one in Canadian Football League with Edmonton, Baker retired from the game and became an attorney.

When Mel's flight to Washington, D.C., to receive the Pigskin Club award was canceled due to fog, he ran into the Dallas Cowboys' personnel executive, Gil Brandt, at the Portland airport. Mel had been introduced to Brandt at age 18 at the Cowboys' first training camp in Forest Grove, Oregon. Brandt, who remained in contact throughout Mel's college years, rented a car to get both of them to the Seattle airport to catch their different flights. Brandt, who would later play a big part in Mel's professional football future, remembered, "The poor kid didn't have $20 in his pocket."

The Pigskin Club trophy was a distinguished award because Mel was recognized for his overall play: running, blocking, passing, receiving, returning kicks, and tackling and intercepting passes. Oregon's U.S. Senator Wayne Morse presented the award to Mel at a banquet of 1,000 at Washington's Statler-Hilton Hotel. When interviewed about professional football, the junior halfback offered: "I have anticipated playing pro ball; I only hope my performance next year will be as good as this year."

Encouraged by the recognition he received, Mel looked forward to his senior season with great anticipation. In the back of his mind, he hoped for another crack at the Beavers and a possible run at the Heisman, if he could stay healthy and not suffer limiting injuries.

12

Senior Season

Mel's track season didn't go as well in spring of 1963. He was hindered by a sore left knee and failed to qualify for the finals.

Even though the "Firehouse Four" backfield of Renfro, Bob Berry, Lu Bain and Larry Hill returned in 1963, Oregon still had their work cut out for them. The Ducks faced yet another strong schedule. But this time, the toughies – Penn State, Washington and Indiana – would all be played in Portland.

Before the season commenced, Mel was honored by being selected as a team co-captain with Hill and Dick Imwalle.

It proved a banner year for junior quarterback Berry as the leader of the team. In addition to a record 16 touchdown passes, he passed for 1,675 yards, allowing only seven interceptions. He added 58 yards rushing for 1,733 yards in total offense.

"Bob was perfect for our team," noted Mel. "He was scrappy and tough as nails. We worked together very well."

Berry in turn was complimentary about Mel. "When I moved Renfro out as a wide receiver, I would ask him, 'Mel, what can you do?'" Berry said. "And he would answer, 'I can do anything you want.' Mel was so athletic, it was just unbelievable what he could do."

1963	(8-3)		
S21	Penn State	L	7-17
S28	@Stanford	W	36-7
O5	@West Virginia	W	35-0
O12	Idaho	W	41-21
O19	@Arizona	W	41-21
O26	Washington	L	19-26
N2	San Jose State	L	7-13
N9	@Washington State	W	21-7
N16	Indiana	W	28-22
N30	Oregon State	W	31-14
D 31	SMU Sun Bowl	W	21-14

After suffering a defensive lapse in the opening 17-7 loss to Penn State, Oregon showed off its backfield speed with big wins over Stanford, West Virginia, Idaho and Arizona. The offense averaged 33 points a game. Then the Huskies came to Portland.

The Washington game was arguably the most brutal and physical game in the rivalry. The Rose Bowl–bound Huskies came to play, winning 26-19. Berry injured his knee and Mel was carried off the field with a cracked rib when he collided at full speed with Washington's Charlie Browning on a kickoff return. The impact echoed throughout Multnomah Stadium.

With both Mel and Berry out, the Ducks got beat by San Jose State (with Berry's brother, Ken, at quarterback), 13-7, at home. The Spartans scored their touchdowns on a punt return and an intercepted pass. The following weekend, Berry limped back on the field to throw two touchdown passes to beat Washington State 21-7.

The Indiana game in Portland found the backfield intact, but not healthy – Berry with a hurting knee, Mel wearing a flak jacket to protect his ribs and Hill in a left-arm brace. Renfro gained 236 all-purpose yards rushing, receiving and returning kicks. Berry threw three touchdown passes – one to Hill, who shook off a tackler with his good arm and scrambled 30 yards for a TD.

Indiana took a 22-21 lead on a field goal with 1:37 left. Berry asked his teammates to "block and give him more time to pass."

The quarterback refused to let the Ducks die. With only 59 seconds remaining, he passed to Renfro; the ball was nearly intercepted, but Mel leaned back, caught it with one hand and gained 30 yards to the Hoosier 38 with 48 seconds remaining. Another pass to Mel gained four. An incomplete pass followed by a defensive offside penalty moved the ball to the 29 with 17 seconds remaining.

Renfro family collection

Co-captain, Hoffman winner and All-American

After the snap, Berry slipped and almost fell before he arched a 40-yard pass to H.D. Murphy down the center behind the Indiana defense for a hard-to-believe touchdown. Oregon scored its first win over a Big-10 opponent 28-22. At 6-3, the Ducks' bowl future depended on winning the Civil War game.

The following week, a series of incidents became a "bump in the road" for Mel Renfro – a large bump.

On Friday, November 22, 1963, there was a stunned reaction to the assassination of John F. Kennedy, the President of the United States. Similar to the December 7, 1941, attack on Pearl Harbor before it and the September 11, 2001, attacks after it, the event shocked the nation. Traffic and work almost came to a standstill. Classes at schools across the country were dismissed. Events were canceled. Many wept while others prayed.

The assassination dissolved differences among people as they were brought together by the shock and sorrow following the shooting of their president in Dallas, Texas. The news hit with such impact that within hours, most of the television sets focused on it. CBS-TV Washington correspondent Roger Mudd summed it up: "It was a death that touched everyone instantly and directly; rare was the person who did not cry that long weekend."

It was no different in Eugene with Mel Renfro.

JFK Assassination Day Accident

"I remember my senior year in high school when Kennedy came through Portland on a campaign swing," recounted Mel. "I was able to see him up close, face to face. It impacted me. Since then, I greatly admired him, he was our president."

The evening of President Kennedy's assassination, after drinking beer with a few of his teammates throughout the afternoon, Mel had a serious accident that almost took his life. Less important, it ended his college career.

"INJURY CLOUDS RENFRO'S GRID FUTURE" screamed the banner headline across the Sunday *Oregonian* sports section.

Don McLeod, the *Oregonian* sports editor, wrote a story detailing that Mel Renfro's college career came to an end by a badly slashed wrist late Friday night. After surgery had been performed, the doctors at Sacred Heart Hospital in Eugene ruled him out of the Civil War game. The game, delayed due to JFK's death, was originally going to be played on November 23 in Eugene, but was moved to the next Saturday, November 30. The injury was too severe for him to play.

Renfro had severed the median sensory nerve and some blood vessels below the wrist of his right hand in the accident. The cut nerve causes a lack of feeling to the thumb, middle and index finger, whereas sliced deep arteries could have been fatal.

In 2013, Mel recounted the details: "I was drinking beer in my apartment with a couple of my teammates during a period I was having a rift with my wife, who was staying with a friend. I didn't go out on the town, as another media report said. All day, I was emotionally upset over the Kennedy assassination. Then my wife unexpectedly showed up in the apartment. It must have upset me. I went into the bathroom and with an emphatic gesture, slammed the bathroom vanity mirror with my hand. My wrist bled badly before teammate Oliver McKinney suggested I go to the hospital. I realize now that probably saved my life."

"I was unable to play the next week," said a remorseful Mel. "That's the way my college career ended."

Ending his college career so abruptly wasn't what the Oregon All-American had hoped. Mel's dream of finishing an injury-riddled senior season with the opportunity to redeem himself from the prior two Civil War losses was disappointing. Mel personally "shouldered" those losses. He considered playing Oregon State his "Achilles heel."

Also lost was the opportunity for a healthy Renfro to turn major bowl officials' heads for his team and to show off his own talent by playing in the East West All-Star Game and the Hula Bowl. But at the time, due to his accident, Mel's physical fitness for professional football was questioned.

Mel led his team in rushing for the third year in a row, gaining 452 yards, averaging 5.5 yards per carry. He caught 18 passes for 260 yards and led the team in scoring with 39 points. Despite not playing in the Civil War and the Sun Bowl, the Oregon co-captain won the team's Hoffman award as its outstanding player, was selected All-Coast for the third year and earned *The Sporting News* and *Time Magazine* first team All-America recognition. Mel was now a two-year All-American in football as well as a two-sport All-American. Meanwhile, a Naval Academy quarterback from Cincinnati named Roger Staubach won the Heisman Trophy.

The Ducks, without their star halfback, won the delayed Civil War game 31-14 behind the brilliant quarterback play and passing of Berry.

"Berry cut the Beavers to ribbons," said future Pro Hall of Famer Dave Wilcox. "They had a special defense for us, and Berry would audible a lot." He passed for a school-record 249 yards and two touchdowns. With the win, the Ducks finished with a bowl-worthy 7-3 record.

But, when Mel was counted out of postseason play, the major bowls looked elsewhere. Finally the Sun Bowl, stepping up as a major college bowl, offered Oregon its bid.

Athletic Director Leo Harris accepted, provided a "suitable opponent" could be secured. That opponent was the Southwest Conference's sixth-place team, Southern Methodist, with a poor 4-6 record. But the Mustangs had beaten Staubach's Navy team, Air Force, Texas A&M and Arkansas while losing close games to Michigan, Rice, Texas Tech, Texas and TCU. To ensure good ticket sales for the Sun Bowl's first year, the game's organizers needed to select a Texas team.

Berry was brilliant again at quarterback, connecting on 11 of 26 passes for two touchdowns as the Ducks won 21-14 to claim the school's first bowl victory since the day of Coach Hugo Bezdek's 1917 Rose Bowl win over Pennsylvania. The bowl game win over SMU, although played in El Paso, might have been considered payback revenge for the 1949 Cotton Bowl loss 15 years earlier between the All-American Norm Van Brocklin–led Webfoot team and the SMU squad led by two All-Americans, Kyle Rote and Doak Walker.

Bob Berry

Bob Berry continued his success into his senior season, leading the Ducks to their third consecutive winning season with a 7-2-1 record in 1964. The Ducks were on a 10-game winning streak going into their last two games. It was also the year the AAWU reinstituted the former Pacific Coast Conference alignment by welcoming in Oregon and Oregon State. The finish was disappointing for the Ducks, who lost both the final game and a bid to the Rose Bowl to Oregon State in the Civil War, 7-6. Berry received national recognition for his play that season. He was named first-team quarterback on the prestigious Kodak All-America team and played in the East-West All-Star Game and Hula Bowl. Although he was drafted by the Eagles after his junior year, he was traded in the 1965 draft to Minnesota. During his 12-year NFL career, Berry played two backup stints with the Vikings before and after his strong five years as a 51-game starter with the Atlanta Falcons from 1968 to 1972, throwing for 8,486 yards and 57 touchdowns. He served as Fran Tarkenton's backup for the last four years with the Vikings before retirement.

Len Casanova

Len Casanova began college coaching in 1936 under the legendary Buck Shaw at his alma mater, Santa Clara. During World War II, "Cas" received a commission and rose to the rank of a U.S. Navy Commander. In 1946, he returned to Santa Clara as its head football coach. His 1948 team defeated Stanford, tied Michigan State and upset Oklahoma in Kezar Stadium 20-17. In 1949, Santa Clara upset the Bear Bryant–coached and heavily favored Kentucky team in the Orange Bowl 21-13. Afterward, when Santa Clara dropped football as a cost-cutting measure, Casanova moved on to University of Pittsburgh for a year, a year when the Korean War draft depleted the number of available players.

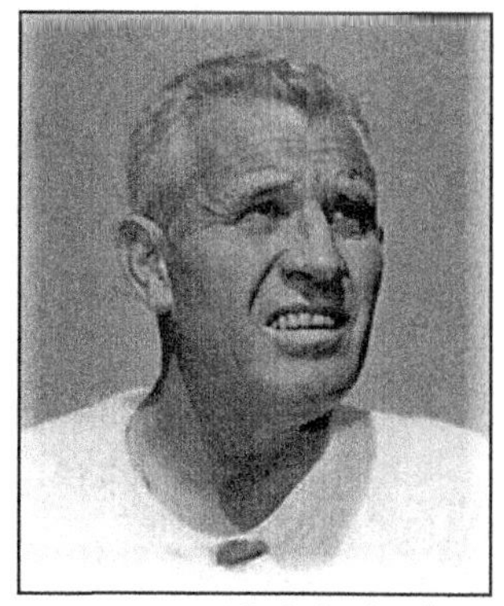

Renfro Family Collection

Len Casanova

Then in 1951, he was hired by the University of Oregon to replace Jim Aiken.

Casanova coached at Oregon for 16 years until 1966, compiling an 82-73-8 record. The highlight was the 1957 PCC co-championship and the 1958 effort in the Rose Bowl, a 10-7 loss to top-ranked and heavily favored Ohio State. Cas became a father figure to his players and coaches. "He was a mentor to all of us, a man who set an example," said reserve end John Robinson, who went on to become a successful coach. "And he loved us and he cared about us as players." John McKay, George Seifert and Robinson began to develop their illustrious coaching careers as assistants under Casanova.

A career 104-94-11 record earned Casanova a 1977 induction into the College Football Hall of Fame as a coach. In 1964, he served as the president of the American Football Coaches Association, and was honored with the Alonzo Stagg award in 1990 for "his outstanding services in the best interests of football." Cas served as the Oregon athletic director from 1967 to 1970, during the time Autzen Stadium was completed. He remained close to the university for years, active in fund-raising efforts and projects to improve the school's athletic facilities. To honor his 40-year contribution and as a legacy to him, Oregon's new athletic department facility was named the Len Casanova Athletic Center. In a 2000 interview, Casanova stated without reservation, **"Mel Renfro was the best football player to play for me on both offense and defense."**

"That was to say a lot," wrote the *Oregonian*'s George Pasero. "Casanova's first All-American at Oregon was the versatile George Shaw in 1954. Shaw as a freshman defensive back on Casanova's first team in 1951 set a single-season school record for interceptions with 13. After that, Shaw played quarterback and sometimes doubled as a receiver."

Said Casanova: "Mel did it all; he could run inside or outside, or make a block. And then there was his defense; he was simply fantastic there."

The legendary coach died in 2002 at age 97.

13

The Pro Draft – The Dallas Cowboys

The uncertainty of the extent of Renfro's injury was a clouded issue in the next couple of weeks, especially for the three professional football leagues that vied for his services. "There was one rumor that Renfro cut off his hand," Dallas Cowboy vice president/player personnel Gil Brandt said. "Some other people said he was paralyzed."

The 1964 National Football League draft was held in Chicago on December 3, 1963.

Before the Oregon football team went to the Sun Bowl, two representatives of the 49ers took Mel and Dave Wilcox to breakfast at the Eugene Hotel. It was the day of the National Football League draft, and three days after the American Football League draft, during which Wilcox was drafted by the Houston Oilers and Mel by the Oakland Raiders. "Bottom line," said Wilcox, "the 49er guys didn't want us talking to any American Football League teams."

"The NFL franchises waited with anticipation as Dallas prepared to make the fourth selection in the first round," reported

Dallas writer Jim Dent. "If Renfro was chosen, his hand must be all right. If not, forget him. The Cowboys waited almost two hours and chose Texas' Outland winner, Scott Appleton. In the second round, though, Renfro went to Dallas, and the long ride began."

In 2012, Brandt reviewed the draft events to get the facts straight.

"Our original intent was to draft Renfro with our first pick the Saturday before his accident," he said. "Because we became apprehensive, it prompted us to have Eugene's Dr. Donald Slocum to check him out. [Although Mel didn't confirm that.] If the injury would have prevented Mel from performing at a high level, we would have drafted Paul Warfield, whom we also had committed to. As it worked out, we drafted Mel with our second pick, No. 17 overall.

"We got caught up with a trade with the Steelers that got us off track drafting Warfield with our first draft pick. Getting future Hall of Famers Warfield and Renfro with the first two draft picks would have been a bonanza for us.

"We knew Houston had offered Appleton a lot of cash, but at the same time, we were working on trading our first pick to the Steelers for their veteran receiver, Buddy Dial. Since our season was still going on and Dial was still under contract, we couldn't announce the trade until later."

However, Appleton signed with Houston of the AFL. The shenanigans the Steelers and Oilers used in their attempts to sign Appleton were some of the favorite stories of Steeler legend, according to broadcaster Myron Cope. It became known as the "Buddy Dial-for-nothing trade." Appleton played for Houston from 1964 to 1966 and the San Diego Chargers in 1967 and 1968.

In the meantime, Mel didn't become aware of his draft status until the ride back with his coaches from the Portland National Football Foundation Scholar-Athlete Banquet.

Brandt, who had the Cowboy draft responsibilities for 29 years, stressed three qualities for each of their selections: character, intelligence and speed. Besides obtaining Dial in the trade and Renfro with the second pick, the Cowboys drafted Georgia Tech quarterback and kicker Billy Lotheridge with their sixth pick. In the seventh round, the Cowboys selected Olympic sprinter Bob Hayes, and as the draft continued into the early morning, they made another future selection that would make a huge impact on the Dallas football franchise. With their 10th pick, Brandt selected the 1963 Heisman winner, Navy's junior quarterback Roger Staubach, whose service commitment would not allow him to be available for five years.

1964 NFL Draft

#	NFL team	Player	Pos	College
1	SF 49ers	Dave Parks	E	Texas Tech
2	Eagles	Bob Brown	OT	Neb.
3	Redskins	Charley Taylor	HB	ASU
4	Cowboys	Scott Appleton	OT	Texas
5	Lions	Pete Beathard	QB	USC
6	Vikings	Carl Eller	DE	Minn
7	Rams	Bill Munson	QB	Utah St
8	Colts	Marv Woodson	HB	Ind.
9	Cardinals	Ken Kortas	T	L'ville
10	Steelers	Paul Martha	HB	Pitt
11	Browns	Paul Warfield	HB	Ohio St
12	Giants	Joe Don Looney	HB	Okla.
13	Packers	Lloyd Voss	OT	Neb.
14	Bears	Dick Evey	T	Tenn
15	SF 49ers	George Mira	QB	Miami
16	Eagles	Jack Concannon	QB	Boston College
17	Cowboys	Mel Renfro	DB	Oregon
18	Redskins	Paul Krause	DB	Iowa

Looking back, the 1964 NFL draft had 11 Pro Football Hall of Famers, more any other class:

Pick	Player	HOF
11th	Paul Warfield	1983
3rd	Charlie Taylor	1984
129th	Roger Staubach	1985
110th	Leroy Kelly	1994
17th	Mel Renfro	1996
18th	Paul Krause	1998
29th	Dave Wilcox	2000
2nd	Bob Brown	2004
6th	Carl Eller	2004
88th	Bob Hayes	2009
89th	Bill Parcells – coach	2013

Signing with the Cowboys

Within hours after the Chicago draft, Brandt signed Lotheridge to a contract and promptly boarded an airplane to Portland to sign Renfro.

"Mel met me at the escalator at the Portland airport," said Brandt. "And when we reached a contract agreement on the drive south to Eugene, we stopped at Corvallis to have the Oregon State football secretary notarize the contact." The agreement was for $20,000, $21,000 and $22,000 the first three years, plus a signing bonus of $20,000 and a new car.

Brandt was quizzed in 2012 regarding what Renfro's drop to the second round might have cost him in salary. "Not much," responded Brandt. "Mel's second round pick in 1963 didn't have much effect salary-wise at all, as it would have years later."

The car was an extra bonus Mel hadn't anticipated. "I went down to the Eugene Pontiac dealer Parmenter Pontiac, and picked out a new pinkish-colored 1964 Pontiac Grand Prix hardtop," he recalled proudly.

Mel and three other Oregon players were drafted by the NFL. Wilcox went to the 49ers in the third round, Berry went in the 11th round to the Eagles as a junior (but signed with Minnesota in 1965) and H.D. Murphy went to the Cowboys in the 19th round.

Renfro was flown to Dallas to meet the media the same week future Cowboy and 1963 Heisman winner Staubach's Navy team lost to Texas 28-6 in the Cotton Bowl. Cowboy owner and founder Bedford Wynne drove Mel around to see the sights around Dallas.

Renfro Family Collection

Gil Brandt signs Mel to Cowboy contract

14

Transition to Pro Football

RENFRO RECOGNIZED IT WAS TIME TO PUT HIS COLLEGE CAREER behind him – time to start the next chapter of his life.

The transition to professional football was immediate. He signed a three-year contract to play professional football with a nice signing bonus that secured his near future. It was also time to move on responsibly, as his wife Pat was pregnant and their first baby was due in January.

Mel didn't enroll for winter term. The University of Oregon's only two-sport All-American, and arguably its greatest athlete, **didn't** graduate from college.

"I was probably a year of credits short," said Renfro. "As only a C student in high school, it was difficult to succeed as a college student while participating in two varsity sports. I remember spending many nights after practice in the library studying and getting tutored. There was no down time for me. I was worn out by the time my career at Oregon came to an end."

Mel had a heartfelt appreciation for how the Oregon coaches treated him. "They were like a second group of parents," he said. "To have them step up and encourage me was important. They always kept on me about going to class and were helpful whenever I needed support. I lived a blessed life, and my wonderful Oregon career was a major part of it.

"Pro football was big! Growing up in Portland, I never envisioned it." In fact, Mel hardly projected college in his future. "I was from a lower middle-class family and we didn't have much money," he said. "You never thought about college and the big-money sports. A lot of my friends were joining the Army or finding jobs in grocery stores."

Vice president/player personnel Gil Brandt was Mel's connection to the Cowboys, although friend Amos Marsh and former UO football and track teammate Mike Gaechter were already on team's roster.

In an extraordinary expression of support, Brandt returned to Oregon in January to help Mel search for and rent an apartment in Northeast Portland in preparation for the arrival of Melvin Jr., who was born on January 25, 1960. Mel needed a place he could bring his family home from the hospital. After a month, Mel packed his prized Grand Prix and headed for Dallas to get acquainted and to rehab his damaged wrist.

As a personal priority, Mel felt it was important for him to pay his respects to his aging and only living grandfather in Houston. "I stopped by Piney Point, which is about 30 minutes out of Houston," recalled Mel. "The personal visit with my grandfather, 'Pappy Jones,' was meaningful. Besides being happy to see me, it was overwhelming to him when I told him about my football contract and the bonus money."

Dallas

Segregation in housing and restaurants became an irritant to Mel when he got to Dallas. He was equally bothered by his new team's racial attitude toward its minority players.

On arrival, the Cowboy management told the black players to

stay out of conflicts and directed them to locate in the apartments in the Oak Cliff district in south Dallas, some 26 miles from the North Dallas practice facility. Mel and Pat moved into the Sutherlin Apartments in Cedar Crest. They joined the other black Cowboy football players – Marsh, Cornell Green, Pettis Norman and Frank Clarke. It made for a lot of camaraderie despite the extended commute to the practice facility. The restaurant discrimination didn't bother Mel. He expected as much. He also remembered the words of his father: "Melvin, don't make a scene; it will only cause you trouble."

"Very few times would I go North Dallas or a white area unless it was a team thing or somewhere we knew we could go," said Mel. "I can remember when the team would go to an area where there was segregation. Coach Tom Landry used to say, 'Fellas, we know what's going on here. We don't particularly agree with it, but that's the way it is, so we have to do what we can do, so we don't create unnecessary problems.'"

Tom Landry and the Cowboys

Although Landry had a five-year contract in 1960, he believed he had to produce a champion in three years or he would be fired.

In 1963, the American Football League Dallas Texans moved to Kansas City. The new Kansas City Chiefs had received a guaranteed 25,000 season tickets by their municipality as a key enticement. The move cleared the local pro football competition for the Cowboys. They would no longer compete head to head for Dallas football fans on Sundays.

Image provided by Steve Liskey - RetroCards.net

Tom Landry

Landry had a plan to build a good defensive team, but he needed to get talented and coachable players who could execute his unique defensive schemes. It took time. Many players were cut, traded or sent on their way when they didn't fit or respect his plan for success. His perceived impersonal approach in the early years was a tough growth period for the young coach, as he slowly replaced the disgruntled retreads with talented young players for the fourth-year NFL expansion team. Though it was against his basic nature, Landry purposely didn't get too attached to players because he was the one to make the face-to-face roster cuts.

The Cowboys struggled the first two months of that season, but they started to win in November, beating the 49ers and the Eagles back to back, before they experienced an emotional setback that affected their play on the field. President John Kennedy was assassinated November 23, 1963, on a ride through the streets of Dallas. Although it stunned the entire country, it was especially devastating to the city of Dallas, the state of Texas, and the Dallas Cowboys for two reasons.

First, it occurred in Dallas at a time President Kennedy wanted to address the civil rights problems of the South. His death was a cruel blow to most of the players – especially the blacks. Secondly, the tragedy haunted the Cowboys for the remainder of the season and into the next. Like the City of Dallas itself, the team would be associated by the rest of the country with the murder of the president.

The 1963 Cowboys finished the season with a 4-10 record, giving Landry a four-year record of 13-38-3.

Many of the Texas sportswriters were critical of Landry for his record and his stoic personality. The writers – and even some of the older players – would have preferred a Bear Bryant or even Bud Wilkinson.

Fortunately for Landry, owner Clint Murchison didn't. Instead of listening to the press and firing his coach, he gave Landry the richest contract in the history of football – a 10-year contract extension after the present one expired at the end of the 1965 season. Murchison valued loyalty and the developmental plan handed off to the triumvirate of General Manager Tex Schramm, Brandt and Landry for the team's future.

After Landry signed the contract, most of the players knew where they stood as Landry proceeded to trim the Dallas roster of its "negative" players.

"When I first met Coach Landry in 1964," remembered Mel, "there were things I noticed about him. He was a man of few words. There was no idle talk. It was always right to the point.

"I began to appreciate his ability to judge talent. My first year, when I had moved to Dallas early to train with some of the veterans, Landry came out to watch some of our drills. I was covering the tight ends in a one-on-one drill in which they couldn't beat me. Coach Landry recognized my defensive skills. Combined with the fact the team was loaded with wide receivers and running backs, he decided to start me at free safety when training camp started in July. I fit in right away. With my skill-set, I immediately started making plays. I felt then, this is going to be fun."

1964 College All-Star Game

Mel's first training camp was at Thousand Oaks, California, on the campus of Cal Lutheran University. It was interrupted when College All-Star Coach Otto Graham contacted the Cowboys inquiring whether their former Oregon All-American was physically fit to be in camp. If he was, the All-Stars wanted him as a running back for their annual summer game against the NFL champions.

"A position change came when I got to Chicago for the pre-game practices," said Renfro. "Arizona State's Charley Taylor was complaining to Graham about playing defense. To help solve the issue, I told Graham that I would play defense. Thus, Paul Krause and I played the corners. I sensed Graham was appreciative and never forgot me after that. He picked me to play in later Pro Bowls when I was selected as an alternate. He told people, 'I want Renfro.'"

The August 7, 1964, College All-Star Game against the Chicago Bears gave Mel his first college all-star game exposure. It allowed him to play with Oregon teammate Dave Wilcox, Ohio State's Paul Warfield, Miami's George Mira, USC's Pete Beathard, Minnesota's Carl Eller, Krause and Taylor, to name a few. Before a Soldier Field crowd of 65,000, former Cleveland Brown quarterback legend Graham coached the All-Stars to a 10-7 halftime lead before losing 28-17 to the NFL champion Bears.

The Chicago Charities College All-Star Classic was a preseason game played annually from 1934 to 1976 (except in 1974) between the NFL champions and a team of college seniors from the previous year. Over the course of 42 games, the NFL champions won 31 games, losing nine to the All-Stars with two ties. The game raised over $4 million for charity. By the 1970s, the pro teams dominated and the interest in the game started to erode. NFL coaches became reluctant for their draftees to miss part of their training camp, and there was a fear of injuries. The final 1976 game was played in such a downpour, it was impossible to perform. Following a game delay, drunk and unruly fans invaded the field and tore the goal posts down. At that time, the sponsor, the Chicago Tribune, Inc., and the NFL Commissioner Pete Rozelle decided the game would be discontinued.

Although Mel missed a couple of weeks of Cowboys' training camp, he made a big impression on defensive coach Dick Nolan by learning the five different coverages in less than a week. "I gave him a test on Thursday, in which he handled it with very few mistakes," Nolan said. "On the field, he had speed, quickness and balance, plus the great knack for running backwards, something a great defensive back has to do to maintain position on the receiver."

The Rookie Season

The Cowboys had hopes for the rookie from Oregon to be an offensive force in the NFL, perhaps as a running back or receiver. But since the team was already loaded at those positions, and because Landry recognized his exceptional talent on defense, Mel started at safety.

After Renfro intercepted a pass in his first exhibition game, Landry utilized his skill-set and expanded him to a three-way defensive player. Not only did Mel replace Warren Livingston at safety, he also took over the punt return duties from Jim Stiger and displaced both Amos Bullocks and Marsh in returning kickoffs.

1964	(5-8-1)		
S12	Cardinals	L	6-16
S20	Redskins	W	24-18
S27	@Steelers	L	17-23
O4	@ Browns	L	6-27
O11	Giants	T	13-13
O18	Browns	L	16-20
O25	@Cardinals	W	31-13
N1	@Bears	W	24-10
N8	@Giants	W	31-21
N15	Eagles	L	14-17
N22	@Redskins	L	16-28
N29	Packers	L	21-45
D6	@Eagles	L	14-24
D13	Steelers	W	17-14

In his 1964 rookie season, Mel Renfro played superbly in four ways:

1. As a pass defender, he had seven interceptions for 110 return yards and a touchdown.

2. As a run defender from the safety position, Mel was credited with tackles saving nine touchdowns.

3. Returning punts, Mel led the NFL with 32 for 418 yards.

4. Returning kickoffs, Mel led the NFL with 40 returns for 1,017 yards. The combined 72 returns for 1,435 total yards in returns were also NFL bests.

Mel was selected to play in his first of 10 consecutive Pro Bowls.

Renfro family collection

Cleveland's Jim Brown

Jim Brown is best known for his exceptional and record-setting nine-year career as a running back for the NFL Cleveland Browns from 1957 to 1965. In 2002, he was named by *Sporting News* as the greatest professional football player ever. At the end of his career, he led the league in rushing a record eight times with 15,549 all-purpose yards and 126 touchdowns. In 2010, Brown was chosen by NFL Network as the second greatest player (to Jerry Rice) in NFL history. Brown retired at 29 and pursued an acting career.

Playing against his boyhood idol was special for Renfro. "I tackled him many times, as hard I could," proudly remembered Mel. "On one play, he ran right over me. But I wrapped his leg until I got some help. On another play, I remember on a 75-yard Brown run, I ran him down at the three-yard line. He told me later I was the only guy who ever ran him down from behind. I played with him in two Pro Bowls."

Pro Bowl

A post-season all-star game called the Pro Bowl, which featured the best players from each of the NFL's two divisions, became a reality in 1951. Later when the rival American Football League merged in 1970, it was officially called the AFC-NFC Pro Bowl. The game was initially sponsored by the Los Angeles Publishers Association, and for many years, the teams would be led by the coach of each of the division champions. The first 21 games of the series (1951–1972) were played in the Los Angeles Coliseum. The site of the game was changed annually for the next seven years before the game was moved to Aloha Stadium in Honolulu for 30 consecutive years from 1980 through 2009. The 2010 game was played at the home stadium of the Miami Dolphins, was held before the Super Bowl and did not include members from the Super Bowl teams. Since 2011, the Pro

Bowls have been played again in Hawaii the week before the championship game.

Renfro's breakout rookie season was extraordinary for a Dallas defensive back. It earned him All-NFL honors and an opportunity to represent himself, the Cowboys and the NFL's Eastern Division in the 1965 Pro Bowl. The opportunity opened up new relationships for him.

"Playing in the Pro Bowl with my idol Jim Brown was inspiring," said a star-struck Mel. "He would pat me on the back and encourage me with, 'Youngster, you will do well in this league.'"

Another experience that impacted Mel was the warm hospitality of Roosevelt Brown. "The huge New York Giant lineman took my wife and me out to dinner and showed us a good time," said Mel. "As a rookie, I was overwhelmed with the amount of money he spent on us."

On game day in front of 60,598 in the LA Coliseum, Mel performed well for the Blanton Collier–coached East squad. He showed off his defensive skills by intercepting a Fran Tarkenton pass in the second quarter and returning it 47 yards for a score.

15

Next Year's Champions

1965	(7-7-0)		
S19	Giants	W	31-2
S26	Redskins	W	27-7
O4	@Cardinals	L	13-20
O10	Eagles	L	24-35
O17	@Browns	L	17-23
O24	@Packers	L	3-22
O31	@Steelers	L	13-22
N7	49ers	W	39-31
N14	Steelers	W	24-17
N21	Browns	L	14-24
N28	@Redskins	L	31-34
D5	@Eagles	W	21-19
D11	Cardinals	W	27-13
D19	@Giants	W	38-20

"Coach Tom Landry had a plan in place to build a winning football team," Mel Renfro said, trying to understand his coach. "One that he believed in, and as the talent got better with more coachable players, his plan came into fruition. Landry was a master strategist, obsessed with detail. He left no stone unturned. When he studied film, he graded every player, offense and defense, on every play. When he broke down the opponent's game film, he did the same thing. I soon realized there was no mystery to why we became consistent winners."

Landry's famed "Flex Defense" made its debut in 1964. By 1965, the defense became effective. In all but three of the 14 games, the Cowboys held the opposition under 24 points. The defense would move from an inside-outside 4-3 into the Flex, giving the defense another look and helping to confuse the opponents' offense.

But micro-managing both his football systems and his players as in a game of chess wasn't the answer for the Cowboys becoming a championship team. There were deficiencies that needed to be addressed. The offense continued to be erratic. Landry began alternating quarterbacks and receivers, trying to find an answer. Defensive tackle Bob Lilly noted another shortage: "We didn't have enough coaches. We had gone three years without having even a defensive line coach. We had just one overall defensive coach, Dick Nolan."

The Emotional Turning Point

Later in 1965, Landry's coaching career reached a positive turning point. It wasn't pre-planned, but the results proved a strong motivation for his struggling team to find a path to become a more consistent winner.

"We won all six of our preseason games, and started the regular season 2-0," said Renfro. "But after losing the next five in a row, we had to re-evaluate who we were. The fifth loss against the Steelers in Pittsburgh was crushing for Coach Landry. He felt he had let us down."

After the loss to the Steelers, Landry emptied the locker

room except for the players and coaches. He began a frank talk, recounting his years of study devising the Multiple Offense and the Flex Defense with the belief the strategies would carry the Cowboys into the future.

"He wanted to thank all of us for giving him 100 percent," wrote Lilly in his autobiography. "He was just crying, and he couldn't control it. He said, 'I very likely won't be around here next year.' With that he just broke down, and boy, we were touched very deeply.

"I think it humbled all of us. From that point on, we were more attentive and much more diligent. We saw a real man up there. We had always taken Coach Landry for granted, and this time we saw a real person. We wanted to fight for him, and we did. I don't think he planned it that way. I know he didn't. It just happened. And I never saw him cry again."

Landry settled on one quarterback, Don Meredith, for the remaining seven games. The Cowboys responded by winning five of them. The 1965 Cowboys finished 7-7 for second in their division. Meredith's passing and the addition of Bob Hayes as a receiver ignited the offense. Hayes caught 46 passes for 1003 yards for 12 touchdowns. He also shared punt and kickoff returns with Renfro, making them a potent tandem.

Mel continued his outstanding play in his second season, earning first team All-NFL again. His 100-yard kickoff return for a touchdown was a highlight, and his kickoff return average of 30 yards remains a single-season Cowboy record. In Mel's second Pro Bowl appearance in January 1966, he seized another defensive opportunity. He picked off another pass, this time from quarterback John Brodie, which he returned 20 yards for a touchdown.

Mel Renfro's House of Sound

Renfro's earliest financial investments were in record shops. The popular black musicians in the 1950s – Chuck Berry, Ray Charles and Fats Domino – helped bring the blues music into the popular music scene.

"When I was in high school, we would buy our music from Clarence Duke's House of Sound in the neighborhood," said Mel. "A few years later, after his store closed, I sought Duke out. He offered me advice and allowed me to use the 'House of Sound' name.

"In the spring of 1966, I opened my first business, Mel Renfro's House of Sound, on a strip mall across from the Franz Bakery on Fremont in Portland. I hired my good friend Cliff Walker as the manager in charge of the little business. We ordered our records from Motown and a San Francisco record wholesaler. The next year, I moved to Dallas full time. Without my participation, Walker grew tired of it and wanted to move on to other things. We moved the business across the street to Willie Harris's building after I sold it to him. I didn't lose any money."

Dickie Daniels

Dickie Daniels, a younger Jefferson High and Cowboy teammate, was a big admirer of Renfro. He would work out with him during the offseason when they were in Portland when Daniels was playing football at Pacific University in Forest Grove. During those workouts, Mel helped him with his technique. Daniels's college play caught the eye of Cowboy vice president/player personnel Gil Brandt and he was signed as a free agent by Dallas in 1966.

Image provided by Steve Liskey - RetroCards.net

Dickie Daniels

Mel remembers encouraging him during a preseason game.

"I told him, 'Dickie, you've got to make a play to show the

coaches you can play at this level,'" said Mel. "Sure enough, he crashed through and made a big hit stopping the 49ers' John David Crow in his tracks during a preseason game."

As a Dallas Cowboy, Daniels experienced an unlikely series of personal events with his head coach that would impact his life's journey in a positive way. He reaped the benefits of the personal side of his mentor.

Daniels made the team as a backup defensive back, a special team member and a kick returner through the 1968 season. He was available when Coach Landry needed a player to demonstrate technique for his three-week clinics throughout the state of Texas.

Landry took a personal interest in his first-year player. "He talked to me a lot about life and about my future," said Daniels in a 2013 interview. "He got me started in my long career as an NFL executive. I owe it to him."

In his second season in the Landry system, Daniels added the responsibility of changing the coverage of the defense for each play. To accomplish this, Landry required him to take home game film each week to study the next week's opponent for its unique differences in how each play was approached. The experiences provided him the basic foundation to understand the Cowboy defensive and offensive concepts.

Daniels saw more of the personal side of his coach than most of Landry's players whom he coached for his 29 seasons. In *Tom Landry: An Autobiography* authored with Gregg Lewis in 1990, Landry attributed not having a closer personal relationship with his players to his "personality shortcomings, demanding perfectionism, emotionally undemonstrative nature and a tendency toward tunnel vision." Landry also believed that because he didn't have a close personal relationship with his players, he "couldn't get them to do what they didn't want to do in order to achieve what they wanted to achieve." Yet Landry's personal relationship with

Daniels still aligned with his basic principle, "to achieve what they wanted to achieve." Daniels received the encouragement and the basic foundation to succeed – first as a coach, then later in the football business.

After joining the Chicago Bears for two years, Daniels was traded to the Miami Dolphins until an early season-ending injury converted into a coaching opportunity. His football knowledge acquired from Landry and the Bears prompted Miami Coach Don Shula to hire him as a coach. It set the foundation for his next career.

Daniels has spent 49 years as a player, coach, personnel evaluator and executive with seven organizations, and he has experienced eight Super Bowls along the way. He is currently with the NFL Football Operations department as a scouting consultant.

1966 MOO (Mel on Offense)

A weakness of the 1965 Dallas team was an inability to run wide. It caused the opposition's defense to gang up on halfback Don Perkins up the middle. Landry decided to move Renfro, his Pro Bowl safety and fine kick returner, to halfback.

Mel, who played offense at Oregon, wanted a shot at either halfback or receiver, and he got it. In the offseason, Landry redesigned parts of the offensive playbook to take advantage of his skill-set. Mel's speed and acceleration gave Dallas a new dimension. The Dallas Cowboy fans and media had even started the "MOO Club," an acronym for "Mel on Offense."

But the experiment was short-lived. Although Mel averaged seven yards per carry in the preseason, he suffered his first injury – a hip pointer. A second injury followed after the regular season started. Mel had eight carries for a 6.5-yard average and caught four passes for 65 yards before he badly hurt his ankle. When Mel healed, Landry moved him back to defense, fearing he might be prone to more injuries.

Said Dallas sportswriter Frank Luksa in a 1996 Pro Football Hall of Fame interview: "My recall of Renfro's regular season offensive career is that it lasted about 10 minutes. He caught a pass from Don Meredith near the Giants' goal line and went down on a tangle of bodies. The Giants' Henry Carr rolled over the back of his leg. The pop Mel heard was a bone chip separating from his ankle, thus ended Renfro's playing days on offense. Once healed, he went back to defense at mid-season and continued his 10 consecutive Pro Bowl credits. Without the injury, he'd have remained a running back of dubious durability."

"I was always getting hit from the blind side because I had a dancing style," said Mel. "I didn't have the strength and power to be a running back. My career would have ended in the next four or five years. Eight years would have been the max, unless they moved me to wide receiver. Then I might have lasted 10 or 12." Had he not been hurt by Carr, Renfro said, his Pro Hall of Fame induction would never have happened.

Landry replaced Mel at halfback with a free agent, a little-known quarterback from South Carolina named Danny Reeves. Reeves was not fast, didn't seem quick, but continually did the things necessary to perform well. He went on to rush for 757 yards, catch 41 passes for 557 yards, and score 16 touchdowns. He also proved an asset with his ability to throw the halfback pass.

1966	**(10-4-1)**		
S18	Giants	W	52-7
S25	Vikings	W	28-17
O2	@Falcons	W	47-14
O9	Eagles	W	56-7
O16	@Cardinals	T	10-10

1966	(10-4-1)		
O23	@ Browns	L	21-30
O30	Steelers	W	52-21
N6	@Eagles	L	23-24
N13	@Redskins	W	31-30
N20	@Steelers	W	20-7
N24	Browns	W	26-14
D4	Cardinals	W	31-17
D11	Redskins	L	31-34
D18	@Giants	W	17-7
	NFL Championship		
J1	Packers	L	27-34

The two NFL Championship games in 1966 and 1967 between the Cowboys and Green Bay Packers pitted two future Hall of Fame coaches against each other: the matchup of the two greatest minds in professional football – Landry and Vince Lombardi.

Landry was the best defensive mind and Lombardi the best offensive coach of their era. From a personality standpoint, they were the opposites of each other. Lombardi was a vociferously demanding coach who would respond with the greatest elation to success and tremendous sadness to the slightest setback. Landry was stoic and calm in even the tense situations.

1966 NFL Championship Game

The talented but young Dallas team had its first winning season in 1966 and was trying to win its first ever world championship. The Packers were a veteran team, enjoying their eighth consecutive winning season under their head coach, and were seeking to win their second consecutive world championship. The Cowboys brought a defensive scheme, "The Flex," which was designed by Landry to stop the Packers' renowned "Lombardi Sweep," a run-to-daylight tactic.

In the NFL Championship Game, the Packers opened with two touchdowns before the Cowboys had the ball. The first was a 17-yard touchdown pass from Bart Starr to Elijah Pitts, and then they capitalized on a Renfro miscue. In one of the rare times in his career extending back to high school, Mel fumbled the ensuing kickoff. Packer Jim Grabowski returned it 17 yards for a touchdown. Before the end of the first quarter, Dallas recovered by scoring two running touchdowns to tie the score.

Mental and leadership breakdowns by the offense at game's end left the home team Cowboys on the short end of the NFL title game with the Packers. In his book, *A Cowboy's Life,* Lilly recounted: "The 1966 Green Bay 34-27 loss, when the Cowboys couldn't score with four chances from the 2-yard line, was the most depressing loss I ever experienced."

The Cowboys were driving for the tying score when the Cowboys called the play that would haunt them for years. Dallas had the ball deep in Green Bay territory, down 34-27. Landry called a short pass to tight end Pettis Norman, who was used primarily as a blocker. Meredith didn't have confidence in Landry's choice of plays, but went with it nonetheless. Norman was wide open on the play. Because Meredith didn't expect Norman in that position, he threw the ball short, causing Norman to run back to catch the ball. That allowed Green Bay to tackle him on the two-yard line. With a more accurately thrown pass, Norman would have jogged into the end zone.

Then Landry, **in a moment unlike him,** lost his concentration on the subsequent play with another ill-advised substitution, sending Bob Hayes in. Hayes was never installed as a blocker. Instead of calling timeout, Meredith sprinted out to the right and was run down by Packer linebacker Dave Robinson, who had brushed past

Hayes. Robinson forced the quarterback to make an out-of-control pass that was intercepted in the end zone.

Two weeks later in Super Bowl I, the Packers beat the Kansas City Chiefs 35-10 in the LA Coliseum.

1967	(9-6-0)		
S17	@Browns	W	21-14
S24	Giants	W	38-24
O4	Rams	L	13-35
O8	@Redskins	W	17-14
O15	Saints	W	14-10
O22	@Steelers	W	24-21
O29	@Eagles	L	14-21
N5	Falcons	W	37-7
N12	@Saints	W	27-10
N19	Redskins	L	20-27
N23	Cardinals	W	46-21
D3	@Colts	L	17-23
D10	Eagles	W	38-17
D16	@49ers	L	16-24
	Division		
D24	Browns	W	52-14
	NFL Championship		
D31	@Packers	L	17-21

1967 "The Ice Bowl"

The Cowboys-Packers rivalry continued into the 1967 season and culminated in one of the classic games of all times – the "Ice Bowl." History notes it was the coldest NFL game in history. It also burned in Lilly's mind, as he explained in his biography: "That morning the temperature was 16 degrees below zero, the coldest New Year's Day in the history of Green Bay."

Lilly said defensive line coach Ernie Stautner wouldn't allow his players to wear gloves.

"The coach groused: 'Men don't wear gloves in this league,'" Lilly wrote.

When the Cowboys went out on the field, all of the Packers' players wore gloves. Because of the horrific conditions that day, Cowboys Renfro, George Andrie, Dick Daniels, Jethro Pugh and Willie Townes were treated for frostbite. Lilly described the 21-17 loss to the Packers as "truly a game of inches."

With the Cowboys leading 17-14, the Packers took over on their own 31-yard line with 4:50 left. On their previous 10 possessions, the most the Packers could advance was 14 yards. But on the final drive, veteran quarterback Bart Starr was at his best. He threw short passes under coverage to Donny Anderson and Chuck Mercein.

The Packers were also aided on a third-down play with a controversial pass interference call on Dave Edwards, in which a pass hit him in the back of his helmet as he was chasing a receiver and he was called for face-guarding. With 16 seconds remaining, Green Bay had the ball, fourth down inside the one-yard line.

The Packers' Jerry Kramer, the key lineman in the winning touchdown play in the "Ice Bowl," framed the event in his book *Instant Replay:* "In the huddle, Bart Starr said, 'Thirty-one wedge and I'll carry the ball.' He was going to try a quarterback sneak. He wasn't going to take a chance on a handoff, or on anybody slipping. He was going to go for the hole just inside me, just off my left shoulder. Kenny Bowman and I were supposed to move big Jethro Pugh out of the way. It might be the last play of the game, our last chance.

"The ground was giving me trouble. The footing was bad down near the goal line, but I dug my cleats in, got a firm hold with my right foot. We got down in position, and Bart called the 'hut' signal.

Jethro was on my inside shoulder, I came off the ball as fast as I ever have in my life. In fact, I wouldn't swear that I didn't beat the center's snap by a fraction of a second. I wouldn't swear that I wasn't offside on the play.

"I slammed into Jethro hard. All he had time to do was raise his left arm. He didn't even get it up all the way before I charged into him. His body was a little high, the way we'd noticed in the movies, and, with Bowman's help, I moved him outside. Willie Townes, next to Jethro, was down low – very low. He was supposed to close to the middle. He was low, but he didn't close. Bart churned into the opening and stretched and fell, landing over the goal line. It was the most beautiful sight in the world, seeing Bart lying next to me and seeing the referee signaling the touchdown." Packers win, 21-17.

Lombardi always preached, "Winning isn't everything, it's the only thing, and you are either first or you're last." Even the Cowboys took it to heart.

Both NFL title games were close losses and huge disappointments for the Cowboys. Winning might have made things different. Had the Cowboys won those games, their confidence might have carried them to future heights. And for their coach, "The Lombardi Trophy inaugurated for the Super Bowl Champions in 1971," noted *NFL Films'* Steve Sabol, "might have been the "Tom Landry Trophy."

On January 14, 1968, in Super Bowl II, the Packers beat the Oakland Raiders 33-14 in Miami's Orange Bowl.

The media tagged Dallas as "Next Year's Champions," while the Packers' second Super Bowl win established them as the premier squad in professional football. It grated on the Cowboys players and their coach. Both games were winnable for them, yet they lost both in the last series of plays.

The Cowboys' 1968 and 1969 seasons ended with Eastern Conference championship losses to the Cleveland Browns. Despite posting the best overall regular-season record for a five-year span – 52-14 – the Cowboys had not made it to the Super Bowl. Whenever they got close, they were unable to climb the final hurdle.

Off the Field

After living in Dallas full time in 1967, Mel opened Mel Renfro's House of Sound in his local neighborhood, in the Wynnewood Village Shopping Mall. "I only had the second business for a year," recalled Mel. "I was talked into musical instruments and some studio-recording which I didn't understand well enough. I felt overwhelmed and got out. I was able to sell it. A Dallas insurance agent Ted Ferguson bought me out and allowed his son run it."

Many of the Cowboys were involved in off-season investments and employment: Craig Morton invested in a bookstore near the campus of the University of California and two sporting goods stores in Davis...they bled dollars...he had to declare bankruptcy; Chuck Howley opened a dry cleaners specializing in uniforms; John Niland opened "King of Barb B-Ques" restaurant; Dan Reeves did public relations with Gifford-Hill Concrete; Willie Townes was a disc jockey in Cliburne; Jethro Pugh was a substitute teacher in Dallas; Pettis Norman was a loan officer at South Oak Cliff State Bank; Bob Lilly and George Andrie ran football camps for kids; Bob Hayes partnered with

Renfro Family Collection

Renfro Family 1968

National Graphics Printing Services selling posters of players; Mike Gaechter opened a janitorial supply store; Jerry Tubbs worked as a loan officer at Dallas Federal and Savings and Loan; Frank Clarke was an equal-opportunity specialist with the Federal Housing and Urban Development; six Cowboys made personal appearances at Sears; while Roger Staubach, who has become the most successful business professional athlete of all time, went to work for Henry Miller Real Estate and Insurance.

16

The '60s and Fair Housing Suit

THERE WERE GROWING TENSIONS IN THE 1960S. THE ROOT CAUSE was our country's involvement in an extended, unpopular and unsuccessful Vietnam War. The draft and large casualty numbers caused frustration and student unrest throughout the nation. It became the "anti-establishment" era. All authority was challenged – parents, teachers or government. Anti-war protest groups caused havoc throughout the nation.

Politically in 1968

An announced 9,000 American soldiers were killed in Vietnam in 1967 (the figure was adjusted in 2013 to 11,363). Casualties rose to a high of 16,899 in 1968.

On March 16, 1968, Robert Kennedy announced his candidacy for president. Two weeks later, Lyndon Johnson announced he would not run for re-election as president.

On April 4, Martin Luther King Jr. was assassinated. Riots swept 100 American cities.

On June 5, Robert Kennedy – who had narrowly defeated Eugene McCarthy in the California primary to become the only anti-war candidate capable of defeating mainstream Hubert Humphrey for the Democratic presidential nomination – was murdered. This time there were no riots, only a pall of sadness. With the deaths of Dr. King and Robert Kennedy, the optimism of the sixties had come to an end.

Since Mel Renfro could relate to both King and Kennedy, his initial response to their deaths was similar to when President John F. Kennedy was assassinated during his senior year in college. This time, Mel carried it to an extreme, and as an employee of the Cowboys, he would later pay the consequences.

"It really tore me apart," Renfro said. "I stayed drunk for a week after the Dr. King assassination. I got real militant and had an attitude, and of course, the Cowboys didn't like that."

Mel felt his indiscretions hurt him when it came time to negotiate his next contract. "Being one of their premier players, they couldn't do anything to me, although they sure wanted to," Renfro said. "So they fixed me by not paying me any money."

Salaries

The Dallas Cowboys organization – with the increased demands of rigid head coach Tom Landry and Tex Schramm's refusal to bring salaries up to league standards – came under attack. The salaries caused frustration and bitterness throughout the team.

Peter Golenbock pointed out in his book *Landry's Boys:* "For the first time, many of the veterans were beginning to question Schramm's loyalty to them, starting to feel strongly that they were being treated unfairly, that the Cowboys were growing rich, that

Tex was growing rich and Landry was growing rich, while they were being doled out crumbs.

"In the era before free agency, Schramm could and did tell a player, 'Take it or leave it.' He could do this because a player had no choice but to negotiate with him if he wanted to play...that not playing would be far worse than playing for a low salary. What made it worse, as part of his negotiation technique, Tex was quick to let the player know that if he didn't like the offer, he could be replaced in a heartbeat."

"We were hearing that from other teams and other players were making good money," said Mel. "The word was getting out that some players were making good money and they didn't have the success the Dallas Cowboys were having: We were America's team and winning big."

Schramm changed course when it came to negotiating Renfro's second three-year contract. Even though the general manager wouldn't allow his players to have agents, he assigned his assistant Bob Ward to deal with Renfro.

"I've heard Larry Wilson of the Cards, a like player, was making $100,000 a year," said Mel. "Here is what I want, $35,000, $45,000, $55,000 on a three-year contract."

"Well Mel, the St. Louis Cardinals pay differently than we do," said Ward, acting like he never heard Renfro's offer. "What do you want?"

"It's right there in front of you," Mel countered.

After staring Renfro down, Ward ended the meeting with: "When you are ready to negotiate, come back and see me."

Mel never talked to Ward again. He was paid, $25,000, $26,000 and $27,000 the following three seasons. With his performance during his initial three-year contract, Mel resented the contract process and compared to others of the same credentials, he felt underpaid. "That's the way they got to me," concluded Mel.

1968 Season

1968	(12-3-0)		
S15	Lions	W	59-13
S22	Browns	W	28-7
S29	@Eagles	W	45-13
O6	@Cardinals	W	27-10
O13	Eagles	W	34-14
O20	@Vikings	W	20-7
O28	Packers	L	17-28
N3	@Saints	W	17-3
N10	Giants	L	21-27
N17	@Redskins	W	44-24
N24	@Bears	W	34-3
N28	Redskins	W	20-17
D8	Steelers	W	28-7
D14	@Giants	W	28-10
	Playoffs		
D21	@Browns	L	20-31
	Losers' Bowl		
	Minnesota	W	17-13

The 1968 Cowboys got off to a hot start winning the first six games and finished with a 12-2 regular season record, the best in the NFL. While 30-year-olds Don Perkins and Don Meredith had great seasons, receivers Bob Hayes and Lance Rentzel were also outstanding. The defense was the league's best. Mel Renfro's safety play earned him the Pro Bowl selection for the fourth consecutive year.

The divisional playoff game against the Browns on December 21, 1968, was devastating. After clobbering Cleveland 52-14 in 1967, Dallas leveled the Browns 28-7 in late September. When the teams met again in December in the playoffs, a Cowboys victory seemed a formality. The heavily favored Cowboys were looking ahead to playing the winner of the Colts-Vikings game for the right to advance to Super Bowl III.

On a muddy Cleveland field, the Cowboys played tentatively through a first half that ended in a 10-10 tie.

Quarterback Don Meredith had passes intercepted on the first two series of the third quarter, leading to two Cleveland touchdowns. The first was a flat pass to Bob Hayes that was picked off for a 27-yard touchdown by Brown linebacker Dale Lindsey. On the next possession Rentzel let a Meredith pass bounce off his hands into Browns' defensive back Ben Davis's hands. On the next play Leroy Kelly ran 35 yards for a touchdown.

Two minutes into the third quarter, Landry panicked and replaced Meredith with Craig Morton, ending all chances the Cowboys had of going to the Super Bowl, as the Cowboys lost 31-20.

Tom Landry told the press, "The Cleveland loss is my most disappointing day as a coach."

Playing in the "Losers' Bowl," matching the teams that failed to advance to the Super Bowl, the Cowboys beat Minnesota 17-13, with Meredith voted MVP. After the game, Meredith, at age 30, ended his nine-year career and retired.

1969 Season

1969	(11-3-1)		
S21	Cardinals	W	24-3
S28	@Saints	W	21-17
O5	@Eagles	W	38-7
O12	@Falcons	W	24-17
O19	Eagles	W	49-14
O27	Giants	W	25-3
N2	@Browns	L	10-42

1969	**(11-3-1)**		
N9	Saints	W	33-17
N16	@Redskins	W	41-28
N23	@Rams	L	23-24
N27	49ers	T	24-24
D7	@Steelers	W	10-7
D13	Colts	W	27-10
D21	Redskins	W	20-10
	Playoffs		
D28	Browns	L	14-38
	Losers' Bowl		
	Rams	L	0-31

In 1969, after the Cowboys drafted Yale running back Calvin Hill, Don Perkins followed Meredith into retirement.

In the spring of 1968, quarterback Roger Staubach had a two-week leave from the Navy to attend Landry's QB school. Landry was inspired by the kind of shape Staubach was in and with his hard-working attitude. He was everything that Landry desired in a quarterback.

When Staubach joined the team in 1969 there was a quarterback controversy. At 27 years of age, he needed and wanted to play. Sitting on the bench behind two veteran quarterbacks was a big concern for him. But within a month a significant change took place: backup quarterback Jerry Rhome was traded. With two quarterbacks on the roster, there was hope for the rookie who had been drafted in 1964 to play.

A Craig Morton injury to his finger in a preseason Jet game gave the untested rookie his first test. Staubach came in and pulled a comeback. In the next preseason game against a good Colt team, he scrambled for 100 yards. Staubach performed well in the season opener against the Cards, hooking up with Lance Rentzel for a 60-yard touchdown for a 24-3 win.

Morton came back the following week against the Saints, then suffered a partial shoulder separation against Atlanta, an injury that continued to hamper him throughout the season. Although he played with pain and lack of passing strength, Morton used the running ability of Rookie of the Year Calvin Hill and that of Walt Garrison. He threw 12 touchdowns to Lance Rentzel. Morton played effectively and skillfully enough in his first year as the Cowboy quarterback to lead his team to an 11-2-1 record.

Consistency

The 1969 season was special for Renfro, who had 10 interceptions and was named first team All-Pro. By mid-season, Landry was uncharacteristically complimentary, calling Mel **"the best in the league at free safety."**

"Only he and I knew how hard I had worked to gain that compliment," Renfro said. "By earning that praise from Coach Landry, the direction of my career was determined.

"He pushed for our team to be consistent and insisted that was the key to winning. If we lost two games in a row, it was pure bedlam. He taught us to recognize the problem immediately. I will always thank Coach for instilling that ethic in me. I always tried my hardest. I remember coming into the Cotton Bowl before an important game when teammate Walt Garrison wished me a good game. He then told me that he didn't need to tell me that because I always played well."

The Cowboys played well until the playoff game with Cleveland. Landry made a strategy switch the week of the game. He switched Mel and Otto Brown back and forth between safety and cornerback trying to cover Cleveland's Paul Warfield. The Browns were successful in isolating Warfield on Brown, shaking the confidence of the Dallas defensive players. Cleveland won 38-14. The players were upset and the press blamed Landry. And for the second year, Landry took it emotionally hard. This time even his coaching philosophies were challenged.

For the "Losers' Bowl" in Miami, the defensive players staged a rebellion of sorts. They had lost confidence in the Flex Defense. They wanted to play defensively the way they desired – by using their natural instincts, rather than reading and reacting to the keys. In a reversal of his tightly held coaching convictions, Landry allowed them to play the 4-3 and play the way they wanted. They lost to the Rams 31-0. The rebellion ended and team challenges remained for 1971.

Renfro's Fair Housing Act of 1968 Suit

By 1969, seven of the Cowboys' 22 starters were black. The race issues the team was dealing with were largely external, beyond the team and the organization.

"In order to have a team that's a unit, to perform together, to stay together, it's got to be off the field, in your every-day life and in all your activities," Mel said at the time. "I don't see much of that here, I can't feel it. I hope for better things – better things for myself, my family and the Cowboys."

For two years, Mel and Pat Renfro sought to live in North Dallas, closer to the Cowboys practice facility. Time after time they were rebuffed.

"In 1969, Pat and I located a duplex from ads in the paper and drove by and saw 'for lease' signs," Renfro said. "We talked to the manager, who said there were four units available and told us we could lease one for $350 a month.

"After Pat and I agreed to live in this nicer place that was near the practice field, Pat went back to make the deal while I flew to

Philadelphia for a game. When she went back to secure the duplex, she found the signs were down. She told me by phone she was informed there were no more units to lease, that they were just for sale.

"I was so upset I could hardly play the game. I later shared with my teammates what had happened. They weren't surprised by it. Many of the black players admitted they had experienced the same thing themselves."

Mel became aware of his civil rights regarding housing.

The Civil Rights Act signed into law in April 1968 – popularly known as the Fair Housing Act – prohibited discrimination concerning the sale, rental and financing of housing based on race, religion, national origin and sex. Intended as a follow-up to the Civil Rights Act of 1964, the bill was the subject of a contentious debate in the Senate, but was passed quickly by the House of Representatives in the days after the assassination of civil rights leader Martin Luther King Jr. The act stands as the final great legislative achievement of the civil rights era.

Attorney Oscar Holcombe Mauzy had heard about the Renfros being refused an apartment rental in North Dallas. Mauzy was a Texas State Senator representing District 23 (Southwest Dallas County) from 1967 to 1986 and the Associate Justice of the Supreme Court of Texas from 1987 to 2002. In the legislature, to which Mauzy dedicated 20 years of service, he was a fierce, honest champion of the underdog. Although he tackled many areas of policy, civil rights and education were dear to his heart.

Mauzy called Renfro. He asked him, "Mel, do you want to fight this?"

"You bet I do!" replied Mel.

"I'll represent you for free," said Mauzy.

"So the two of us sat down and talked about it, and we filed a suit in federal court," said Mel.

Emboldened by his stature as a star player for the Cowboys and the encouragement of the state senator who would represent him,

Renfro became the plaintiff of the **first** Civil Rights Fair Housing suit in the State of Texas. He felt in his heart it was the right thing to do.

"But when the Cowboys found out I was taking it to court, Tex Schramm called me into his office," recounted Mel. "For 35 to 40 minutes he hammered me: 'Mel, you can't do this! This is going to hurt you.'"

"But I've been hurt by being denied housing," Renfro told Schramm.

When the Cowboys general manager sensed his All-Pro defensive back couldn't be deterred from going forward with the Civil Rights suit, he reversed his opposition. He offered Renfro full support from the Dallas Cowboy organization.

"I'm with you all the way!" he said. It was a false promise. A Cowboy representative never showed at the trial. Schramm didn't want to appear on the wrong side just in case the Renfros won their case. Afterward, Mel even had to rebut the media claim that Mauzy was hired by the Cowboys.

"I found out later that Schramm was afraid of the white hierarchy in Dallas, the real estate business," declared Mel. "There was pressure on him to have me not pursue this, because a winning suit would drastically affect real estate."

On October 14, 1969, two days after the Cowboys won a close game with the Falcons, Renfro petitioned the federal court to order the Executive Duplex Apartments at 6135 Rencon Way in North Dallas to stop discriminating against Negroes, a violation of the Fair Housing Act of 1968.

It was Mel's first exposure to the court system.

"The case was long and drawn out," said Mel. "It was really hard for me to experience. Their attorneys badgered me to say things that could discredit me, although there were many trick questions I didn't need to answer. Supposedly the real estate people spent a lot of time and money trying to destroy my story: 'I went to lease this apartment and they denied me.' They asked, 'Why did they deny you?' I answered, 'Because I was black.'"

"The judge was Sara Hughes," said Mel. "She knew what was going on, but she had to act like a judge."

But the law prevailed. Renfro won the case and $1,500 in damages; he was offered another duplex. The owner of the apartment complex in North Dallas said, "Take your pick, you can move into any unit you want."

Due to the negative publicity from the trial that revealed the location of the complex, the Renfros moved another half-mile away to avoid any incidents. Their daughter Cindy was a baby, while Tony was three and little Melvin was now four.

From that point, the doors opened to minorities in the housing industry in Texas. Mel received a lot of supportive mail afterward, including a few letters from mixed couples who faced similar housing discrimination problems.

Mel felt Schramm, who represented the business side of the Cowboys, resented his actions to proceed with the suit and held it against him by not paying him a salary commensurate with other star players in the league who played the same position.

17

Blooper Bowl to Pro Bowl MVP

The 1970 Season

1970	(10-5-0)		
S20	@Eagles	W	17-7
S27	Giants	W	28-10
O4	@Cardinals	L	7-20
O11	Falcons	W	13-0
O11	@Vikings	L	13-54
O25	@Chiefs	W	27-16
N1	Eagles	W	21-17
N8	@Giants	L	20-23
N16	Cardinals	L	0-38
N22	@Redskins	W	45-21
N26	Packers	W	16-3
D6	Redskins	W	34-0
D12	@Browns	W	6-2
D20	Oilers	W	52-12

1970	(10-5-0)		
	Playoffs		
D26	Div. – Lions	W	5-0
J3	NFC – @49ers	W	17-10
	Super Bowl V		
J17	Colts	L	13-16

By 1970, pro football had become the country's most popular spectator sport because of television. As the franchises made more money, the players wanted better salaries, more flexibility to change teams and the ability to hire agents.

In Dallas, football coach Tom Landry demanded loyalty and dedication in 1970. Even though running back Calvin Hill had been the NFL rookie of the year in 1969 and finished second in the league in rushing, the Cowboys drafted Duane Thomas from West Texas State College with their No. 1 choice. Hill had been told his role was going to be expanded. Now he was confused and angry.

Landry's increased demands of the players and general manager Tex Schramm's stubborn refusal to bring salaries up to league standards began to build a groundswell of bitterness among the Cowboy players.

Mel Renfro was included in this group.

The Players' Strike of July 1970

The NFL Players Association began negotiating a new collective bargaining agreement with the owners' negotiating committee, which was headed by Schramm.

The veteran Cowboy players voted to strike. They didn't go to training camp in Thousand Oaks, California. They stayed in Dallas and worked out at SMU.

The NFLPA negotiated for players while Schramm represented

the owners. Schramm was uncompromising. When the collective-bargaining agreement was settled in August, Schramm gloated, "The players got very little for their efforts." Schramm won most contract negotiations with his players, allowing the organization to save money so the owner could finish his construction project, the Texas Stadium at Irving – skyboxes and all.

It was not uncommon for Schramm to have disagreements with players, which would result in intimidating threats with long-range consequences. His business style was to solve most player issues and salary dealings with his "sit down, one-on-one style."

Lee Roy Jordan's tough experiences were one example. The two time all-pro linebacker, whose career spanned from 1963 to 1976, had ongoing problems with Schramm, especially late in his career. In 1973, Jordan and all-pro defensive tackle Bob Lilly stood their ground in salary negotiations by missing practices. Cowboy general manager Schramm was furious.

Lilly got his contract worked out quickly and to his satisfaction, but Jordan's holdout was different. He practiced and played hard until the final cuts were made and the regular season started. Then he began a holdout. It left the Cowboys without a middle linebacker. Landry and Schramm got together. Within three days, Jordan signed a $75,000 contract with bonus clauses totaling $100,000. Even when Jordan had an all-pro season, Schramm didn't forget or allow him to forget their confrontation. The player who had been a "tackling machine" for 14 seasons was not inducted into the Cowboy Ring of Honor until after new owner Jerry Jones took over and Schramm had left the organization. Jordan's induction in 1989, at the behest of Lilly, came 13 years after his retirement.

Renfro's Move to Cornerback

In 1969, the Cowboys' secondary gave up 2,657 passing yards and an unacceptable 23 passing touchdowns, more than any of the other division winners. "That's too many," concluded Landry. "We're going to shake up the defensive backfield."

In a calculated move, he shifted all-pro Renfro, his six-year safety whose 10 interceptions led the NFL in interceptions in 1969, to the right cornerback position. The move allowed Cornell Green to slide over to strong safety and Mel to match up with the late addition of former Green Bay Packer Herb Adderley at the cornerback spots. Free agent Cliff Harris beat out third-round draft pick Charlie Waters for the free safety job.

"Truthfully, I would rather play safety, but I will go anywhere to help straighten out our problems back there," said Mel at the time. "The corner is a real challenge. You're closer to the action and your responsibilities are a little different. For instance, you have to crash and take out the interference on a sweep."

Having learned his cornerback technique by studying Green, who had played cornerback his first eight seasons, Renfro became a solid "shut-down" cornerback, forcing the Cowboy opponents to honor him due to his ability to break up or intercept most passes thrown his way. His interception numbers declined after he became a cornerback because opposing teams were reluctant to throw in his direction. During one season, the opposition completed only six of 36 passes thrown in Mel's area in the first 10 games. "I wished they would throw at me," Mel complained. "It hurts you when they don't, because when you are watching a receiver, you should anticipate what they are going to throw to him on every play. When they don't, you tend to get a little complacent."

But there was a positive aspect to the move to cornerback in Renfro's view. "During the six years I was a free safety," said Mel, "I was always beat up after a game and sore for a couple of days later. Since I switched to corner in 1970, there were Sundays when I went to the dressing room feeling like I hadn't played at all."

Herb Adderley

Adderley, a NFL all-pro star disgruntled with Vince Lombardi's coaching replacement Phil Bengtson, was traded to the Cowboys late in the preseason of 1970 by an unusual set of circumstances. Adderley wanted to be traded to home-town Philadelphia or even to the Redskins. But in defiance of his wishes, he was traded to the Packers' rival of the '60s, the Dallas Cowboys, a team now rumored to be experiencing racial problems and having a stingy payroll compared to most NFL teams.

Despite Landry's reluctance to have a former Green Bay Packer on his team, Herb Adderley's influence brought a necessary winner's attitude to the Cowboys. They were referred to as "next-year's champion" after losing two bitter defeats at the hands of Green Bay and back-to-back games at the hands of Cleveland. Adderley's verbal encouragement backed up with strong cornerback play helped get them to two Super Bowls during the three years he wore the Cowboy uniform. "I helped them both on and off the football field to get to two Super Bowls, and the Cowboys beat the Packers for the first time in a 1970 regular season game, my first year with Dallas," Adderley was quoted in his 2012 book *Lombardi's Left Side.*

On November 16, the Cowboys suffered a humiliating 38-0 home loss to St. Louis on Monday Night Football to fall to 5-4 as hopes for a return trip to the playoffs looked bleak. Even Landry expressed his low expectations for his team: "I didn't expect us to win."

The negative attitude bothered the players, but it was Adderley who was the most disturbed. Renfro said, "Our guys were sitting around with their heads down and Herb just exploded. He said, 'What in hell is wrong with you guys? You act like a bunch of losers.' The whole locker room got a wakeup call. Herb got our attention."

A team meeting without the coaches was called. "Nobody is pulling for us," said Lee Roy Jordan. "We're going to do it for ourselves." With Adderley interjecting the needed emotional encouragement, the players' intensity went up in practice, which was reflected in the next win over Washington 45-21. Football became fun again for the team as the players got more involved in the game plans. The Cowboys finished the regular season 10-4, winning the final five games and the Eastern Division.

When Herb became Mel's roommate in camp and on the road, Herb tagged him, "Brother Fro." The opportunity became an awareness experience for Mel. He had been perplexed and always felt, "The Packers would always beat us, but we were the better football team." It bothered him until Adderley had him understand the striking contrast of the coaching styles of the two head coaches and why the Packers **were** the better team.

The Lombardi teams were always prepared and inspired by their coach for the games. After the Packers took the field, their coach was on the sidelines, and the game was for the players to win or lose.

The Cowboy teams were prepared too, but they were led by their stoic cerebral coach with his defined systems of play. Landry demanded control of their play on both sides of the ball from the sidelines. His players were essentially treated like robots.

Lombardi's greatness was the Packers' ability to win close championship games. The Cowboys played just well enough to lose.

The Playoffs

Renfro made two of his biggest plays in the 1970 playoffs. The Cowboys were leading the Detroit Lions 5-0 at the Cotton Bowl with a safety and a field goal while their offense was unable to turn 209 yards of total offense into more points.

With seconds remaining and the Lions driving, Mel intercepted an overthrown Billy Munson pass intended for Earl McCullouch. The pass was high, causing McCullouch to jump while tipping the ball. Mel had backed off and made a dive for the ball. He snared it, hauling it in at the Dallas 17, to preserve the 5-0 win. Mel recalls the elation when the game was over with sideline accolades: "Way to go, Mel. Way to go, Mel." The most exciting game of Mel's career was the Lion game...then the 49er game, and then Super Bowl V.

The next Sunday against San Francisco in Kezar Stadium in the second round of the playoffs, Mel made another interception in the third quarter that helped preserve a 17-10 victory.

"As they were driving, quarterback John Brodie was going deep to Gene Washington," said Mel, who had led the league the previous season with 10 interceptions. "I was thinking about losing the previous four years in the playoffs, and there we were again. I intercepted it and brought it back a few yards, breaking their backs. There wasn't a better feeling knowing **we were no longer next year's champions.** Those two wins put us into our first Super Bowl."

Said Walt Garrison to his teammate, "Mel, your interceptions gave me enough money to buy a new truck."

The Dallas pass defense gave up only 1,913 yards and 10 touchdowns through the air through the Super Bowl. With just 10 rushing touchdowns allowed, "Doomsday" (see Chapter 19) did its part as the Cowboys marched through their schedule to Super Bowl V.

Super Bowl V

Sunday, January 17, 1971

@Orange Bowl	1	2	3	4	Final
Dallas Cowboys	3	10	0	0	13
Baltimore Colts	0	6	0	10	16

MVP Chuck Howley

The Tipped Pass

The second-quarter play in Super Bowl V that gained the media's attention was the alleged tipping or changing of the trajectory of a pass from Baltimore's Johnny Unitas to John Mackey. The alleged "tipper" who facilitated the touchdown may have been wide receiver Eddie Hinton.

The overthrown or high pass was behind Hinton when cornerback Renfro jumped to defend the pass. Mel didn't feel the sensation of touching the football. The ball fell into the arms of Mackey, who completed the play for a 75-yard touchdown.

Although Mel complained to the officials he didn't touch the ball in flight, they ruled otherwise. A tipped ball by a defender allows another receiver to legally catch the ball. If Hinton had tipped the pass to Mackey, the touchdown would have been called back. The controversial play tied the score 6-6, after which Jim O'Brien missed the extra point attempt.

The disputed play dominated the post-game write-ups, but didn't reflect the poor offensive execution of both teams in Baltimore's 16-13 win at the Orange Bowl. Mel assumed some of the responsibility: "It was the job of the free safety to cover Mackey."

A Super Bowl record 11 combined turnovers gave the game a better descriptive title: "The Blooper Bowl."

Afterward, Lilly ripped off his helmet in frustration and tossed it 40 yards downfield. Dallas linebacker Chuck Howley refused to accept the MVP award, commenting, "It doesn't mean anything to me if we lost the game."

"Why did you lose Super Bowl V for us?"

Mel had just boarded the Cowboy office building elevator and to his surprise was confronted by owner Clint Murchison with, "Why did you lose the Super Bowl for us?"

"How could he make that accusation to single me out?" Renfro said much later. "It devastated me. What bothered me also was I had such little contact with Mr. Murchison. We hadn't exchanged 10 words in my entire career with the Cowboys.

"The tipped ball play had nothing to do with the outcome of the game. After the touchdowns the game was tied 6-6. Besides, I made a significant interception in that game – a second-quarter Johnny Unitas pass intended for Hinton. It stopped a drive on [the Cowboys'] 15-yard line while we were leading 13-6."

Later in the game, with the score tied 13-13, Dallas QB Craig Morton threw a pass off the hands of Dan Reeves that was intercepted by Mike Curtis, who ran the ball back to the Dallas 28 with about a minute left in the game. With 5 seconds left, Jim O'Brien kicked a 32-yard field goal for a 16-13 win.

NFL owners often become emotional with winning and losing football games because they have so much invested in their product. Losing a Super Bowl might compound the feeling. An owner may be entitled to those expressions of frustration as the one directed at Mel. But Murchison's comment bothered him for years.

Super Bowl V, Mel Renfro: The Allegations Stop Here

In 2007, during Pro Football Hall of Fame week in Canton, Ohio, Dr. Kristine Setting Clark, a football feature writer and author, sat down with Renfro to set the record straight.

Concluded Renfro: "The Cowboys reviewed the tipped-ball play a thousand times and it came up the same each time – inconclusive. With 11 combined turnovers, a slew of penalties and the knowledge that there was never any conclusive evidence that I had touched the ball, let it be known that **the Cowboys' loss in Super Bowl V was solely due to a culmination of the team's poor field performance, sloppy plays and horrific referee calls.**"

Pro Bowl's Most Valuable Player Back Award

Mel was still seething from his team's Super Bowl loss and the negative media attention he personally received over the "tipped-ball" play when he arrived in Los Angeles the following week for the Pro Bowl. His play in the all-star game exemplified his competitive nature. It helped atone for the loss and set the stage for the following season.

Renfro's seventh Pro Bowl performance on January 24, 1971, before 48,222 L.A. Coliseum fans was his finest.

The game was the anticipated first matchup between the National Football Conference (NFC) and the recently merged American Football Conference (AFC, formerly the AFL). It pitted 49ers coach Dick Nolan of the NFC against Raiders coach John Madden of the AFC. Nolan was previously Renfro's secondary coach with the Cowboys.

"I was trying to avoid answering questions from the media about the Super Bowl," Renfro said. "Coach Nolan abruptly informed me: 'Snap out of it, Mel. You're also going to return kicks this week.'"

Renfro Family Collection

1970 Pro Bowl MVP

While the NFC's defense dominated throughout the game, Mel lit up the scoreboard with two explosive plays. In the fourth quarter, Mel fielded a line-drive punt from Jerrel Wilson of the Chiefs, broke free and returned it 82 yards for a TD. Later, Wilson boomed a 52-yard punt and again Mel fielded it on a full gallop. He moved to his left, then cut right and returned it

56 yards for the score. The final tally was 27-6, a convincing NFC victory.

Mel was honored as the most valuable back of the game, while Fred Carr of the Packers was the most valuable lineman.

Renfro played in 10 consecutive Pro Bowls (1965–1974) and is the **only** player in its history to play safety and cornerback and return punts and kickoffs.

18

Super Bowl VI Champions

1971	(14-3-0)		
S19	@Bills	W	49-37
S26	@Eagles	W	42-7
O3	Redskins	L	16-20
O11	Giants	W	20-13
O17	@Saints	L	14-24
O24	Patriots	W	44-21
O31	@Bears	L	19-23
N7	@Cardinals	W	16-13
N14	Eagles	W	20-7
N21	@Redskins	W	13-0
N25	Rams	W	21-15
D4	Jets	W	52-10
D12	@Giants	W	42-14
D18	Cardinals	W	31-12
	Playoffs		
D25	@Vikings	W	20-12
J2	49ers	W	14-3
	Super Bowl VI		
J16	Dolphins	W	24-3

The most important season in the first dozen years of the Dallas Cowboys' franchise was 1971. The team had hurdles to clear, both psychologically and physically.

The Cowboys entered the season still haunted by having the reputation of "not being able to win the big games." The prior season's Super Bowl V loss added fuel to that view.

There was great anticipation for the new Texas Stadium at Irving, which was initially supposed to open for business at the start of the 1971 season but wasn't ready until October 24. The earlier home games that season were played at the Cotton Bowl.

Texas Stadium at Irving

Dallas Cowboys owner Clint Murchison and president Tex Schramm announced in 1967 plans to build a new stadium owned by the city of Irving, Texas, a suburb of Dallas. "Texas Stadium" was to have a seating capacity of 65,675 and feature 175 luxury boxes called the "Circle Suites," which provided the team with a large new income source exempt from league revenue sharing. Each unit had instant replay, closed circuit television and 256 square feet of "personal privacy and prestige," which included two rows of six comfortable seats and a wet bar. During the first season, men dressed in suits while women went semiformal, many with mink coats. The occupants amused themselves playing bridge, quaffing drinks and ordering snacks from their private waiters while eyeing the action of the other suites. They were worlds away from the boisterous crowds associated with the game of football. Pat Toomay dubbed the occupants "the Romans," while Joe Patoski's book, *The Dallas Cowboys,* noted Don Meredith's observation: "There was mixed response to the suites and stadium, which some people described as the finest facility in football while others called it a vulgar display of wealth. Both were considered attributes in Texas." The most distinctive element of Texas Stadium was its partial roof. Said Cowboy linebacker

D.D. Lewis, "Texas Stadium has a hole in the roof so God can watch his favorite team play." In 2009, the stadium was replaced by the AT&T Stadium in Arlington, Texas.

Mel Renfro was quoted in Peter Golenbock's book, *Landry's Boys,* as saying this about the new stadium: "I loved the Cotton Bowl...loved it. My only feeling about Texas Stadium was that we *had* to go. It was very disappointing to me, because it eliminated a lot of black Americans from attending the games. It eliminated the crowd excitement and its noise. It was just different – like you were playing in your living room. It seemed like a bunch of rich people who couldn't get excited about anything. It was just a totally different atmosphere. I didn't like the move at all."

Another hurdle was the team's slow start and a quarterback controversy. The 1971 season started with Coach Tom Landry alternating Roger Staubach and Craig Morton. But the Cowboys stumbled out of the blocks and were 4-3 at the season midway point before the coach settled on Staubach.

"Roger was different," recalled Mel. "He didn't fear the close games. With Roger at the helm, we looked forward to them. With our relentless defense, together with Duane Thomas's running and Roger's passes, we couldn't be stopped."

The Cowboys won their last seven regular-season games to finish with an 11-3 record. They defeated the Minnesota Vikings and the San Francisco 49ers in the playoffs to reach the Super Bowl. Their opponent, the Miami Dolphins, was making its first Super Bowl appearance with a 10-3-1 regular season record, which included eight consecutive victories and postseason wins over the Kansas City Chiefs and the Baltimore Colts.

Viking Playoff Game

The first-round playoff game with the Vikings was at Metropolitan

Stadium in Bloomington. Game-time temperature was 31 degrees. Although the Vikings outgained Dallas 311-183, the Cowboys converted turnovers into 13 points toward a 20-12 win. A Cliff Harris interception in the third quarter set up Thomas's 13-yard touchdown run. Staubach's nine-yard TD pass to Bob Hayes completed the scoring.

NFC Championship Win over the 49ers

On January 2, 1972, the NFC Championship game was staged at the new Texas stadium in Irving, and the Cowboys' Doomsday Defense prevailed. The defense dominated the 49ers' offense by allowing only nine first downs and 61 rushing yards while forcing three interceptions.

A George Andrie interception of a John Brodie screen pass with a seven-yard return to the 49er two-yard line set up a Calvin Hill touchdown run in the second quarter. With 6:52 remaining in the third quarter, Brodie's 24-yard completion to Ted Kwalick set up a Bruce Gossett 28-yard field goal for the 49ers' only score.

Following a missed Gossett 47-yard field goal, Staubach engineered a 14-play, 80-yard drive with Duane Thomas's two-yard touchdown run making the score 14-3. The Cowboy defense took over the rest of the game forcing turnovers on the 49ers' last three drives, earning their trip to Super Bowl VI.

Before the Super Bowl game against Miami, Mel noted with confidence, "We knew we were going to win."

Super Bowl VI

Sunday, January 16, 1972

@Tulane Stadium	1	2	3	4	Final
Dallas Cowboys	3	7	7	7	24
Miami Dolphins	0	3	0	0	3

MVP Roger Staubach

Super Bowl VI was played January 16, 1972, at Tulane Stadium in New Orleans in front of 81,023 fans in 39-degree weather. A load of 20,000 balloons was released and eight F-4 Phantom jets flew over the stadium as the Air Force Academy Chorale sang the national anthem.

Ray Scott and Pat Summerall announced the game before an estimated 56 million television viewers. The cost of a 30-second commercial was $86,000.

The Dolphins were a very young team with a punishing running attack that was led by Jim Kiick and Larry Csonka, while quarterback Bob Griese led the passing attack. Warfield, possibly the best wide receiver in the league, was Griese's favorite target.

Renfro's move to cornerback produced a classic duel between him and Miami's talented receiver. "Against the Dolphins, Coach Landry used the KISS theory...**keep it simple, stupid,**" said Mel. "We knew we had to eliminate Warfield. Since our linebackers could cover their tight ends, it allowed us to double-team their wide receivers. Our defensive linemen, especially Bob Lilly, were all over Griese all day. That was the key."

Shortly before Super Bowl VI, President Richard Nixon weighed in on some pregame discussion. He telephoned Dolphin coach Don Shula to suggest a particular pass play. "Throw the ball to Warfield on the slant play," he advised. The play was attempted in vain. Three times Mel jammed the play. Warfield was limited to four receptions for 39 yards and did not score.

Paul Warfield had been selected with the 11th pick in the first round of the 1964 draft by the Cleveland Browns. The running back from Ohio State was used as a wide receiver in his 14-year professional career. In his 13 NFL seasons, eight with the Browns and five with the Dolphins, Warfield caught 427 passes for 8,565 yards for a 20.1-yard average and 85 touchdowns. In his 1975 World Football League season with the Memphis Southmen/Grizzlies he caught 25 passes for 422 yards, a 15.9 average and three touchdowns. Warfield was a Pro Bowl selection eight times, a two-time Super Bowl champion (VII, VIII) and a member of the NFL's 1970 All-Decade team. He retired in 1977 and was inducted into the Pro Football Hall of Fame in 1983.

The Cowboys received the first big break near the end of the first quarter of Super Bowl VI when Csonka, who had not fumbled all season, missed a handoff from Griese. Dallas linebacker Chuck Howley recovered the fumble at the Cowboys' 46-yard line. The ensuing drive turned into a Mike Clark nine-yard field goal to go up 3-0.

In the second quarter, the Cowboys marched 76 yards in eight plays, culminating when Staubach hit Lance Alworth for a seven-yard touchdown pass for a 10-0 lead. With four seconds remaining in the first half, the Dolphins got on the scoreboard with Garo Yepremian's 31-yard field goal.

The Cowboys took the second-half kickoff and moved 71 yards in eight plays for a Duane Thomas three-yard touchdown to take control of the game. Howley's fourth quarter interception of a Griese pass with over 11 minutes to play was returned 41 yards to the Miami nine-yard line before Staubach hit Mike Ditka for the 24-3 final score. The Doomsday Defense held tough and the Cowboys won their first Super Bowl.

"Happiest I've ever been as an athlete," said Renfro after he hugged Landry coming off the field. "We hoisted our smiling coach on our shoulders and carried him around. We were very joyful. It felt great. We finally got the monkey off our back about not being able to win the big game the previous five years. We were finally Super Bowl Champions."

A big star of the victory was Thomas. He carried the ball 19 times for 95 yards against a tough Dolphin defense led by Nick Buoniconti, but may have excluded himself from MVP consideration for his distracting and unconventional pre-game week behavior.

As the voting turned out, Staubach received the award and the

Corvette that went with it. He had his usual good game, completing 12 of 19 passes for 119 yards and two touchdowns. Super VI was Thomas's last game with the Cowboys. Said Landry of Thomas: "He was a reflection of the social revolution of the '60s." Thomas came back for a tryout in 1976, but was cut in training camp.

19

Doomsday Defense I 1966–1971

Year	Win-Loss	Score pts	Allowed	Diff	Take / TO	Rush TD	Pass TD	Rush yards	Pass yards	Results
1966	10-3-1	445	239	206	+7	6	17	1170	2382	NFL loss to Packers
1967	9-5-1	342	268	74	+6	11	21	1081	2790	NFL loss to Packers
1968	12-2-0	431	186	245	+8	2	20	1195	2438	Div loss to Browns
1969	11-2-1	369	223	146	+5	3	23	1050	2657	Div loss to Browns
1970	10-4-0	299	221	79	+11	10	10	1656	1913	Super Bowl V loss
1971	11-3-0	406	222	184	+16	8	15	1144	2324	Super Bowl VI win

Total 63-19-3

- Won 75% of all games
- 1971 – Won last 10 games, gave up 95 pts, 9.5 pts/game; 755 yards rushing, 75.5 yards per game

The Doomsday Defense was more than just a group of good football players. The group was the backbone of a team of determined warriors striving to secure a goal that eluded them for five seasons – to win the Super Bowl. They were led by an extraordinary coach who believed that preparation was a team's the greatest motivator.

Mel Renfro was captured in a classic picture hoisting a smiling coach Tom Landry on his shoulders after winning their first Super Bowl by beating the Miami Dolphins 24-3. He later related that "Winning Super Bowl VI was the greatest accomplishment of my athletic career."

Fred Goodwin, a Dallas Cowboy historian, said the term "Doomsday Defense" was created by the media of the 1960s. It was just one of many during that era, including the Los Angeles Rams' "Fearsome Foursome" Front Four of Lamar Lundy, Rosie Greer, Merlin Olson and Deacon Jones; the Minnesota Vikings' "Purple People Eaters" Front Four of Alan Page, Carl Eller, Jim Marshall and Gary Larson and the Pittsburgh Steelers' "Iron Curtain" Front Four of Joe Greene, L.C. Greenwood, Ernie Holmes and Dwight White.

The original Doomsday Defense can generally be identified as the Cowboys' defensive unit of the 1966–1971 seasons. Doomsday II had its heyday from approximately 1977 to 1982. Perhaps the biggest difference from the other teams was the Cowboys' nickname was inclusive of the 11 defensive players, not just the front four linemen.

Being part of Doomsday meant a lot to Renfro. It identified him with the strong legacy of the first Dallas Cowboys dynasty. The Doomsday Defenses were the strength of the Cowboy teams that won two Super Bowls and played in three more.

"One reason I believe 'Doomsday I' was so good was because we got to know each other so well," recalled Mel. "Most of us played together for at least six years. Players don't do that anymore; they're constantly moving from team to team. Bob Lilly, George Andre, Jethro Pugh, Larry Cole, Lee Roy Jordan, Dave Edwards, Chuck Howley, Cornell Green and I saw the same faces each year. We got to know each other well."

DB Mel Renfro 1964–77

Image provided by Steve Liskey - RetroCards.net

Mel Renfro

Renfro, nicknamed "Suds" for his penchant for beer, "Bro Fro" or just "Fro" by his teammates, was an important cog of the Cowboys' defensive success due to his performance as a safety and later as a "lock-down" cornerback.

"I had a tremendous ability to run backwards, and I could also high jump 6-6," added Mel. "Over time, I also became skilled at reading offenses by watching the quarterback's eyes."

In practice, teammate and receiver Frank Clarke had to scrimmage against Mel often. He raved about him. He was quoted in Peter Golenbock's book, *Landry's Boys:* "Mel was so good. Man, yes, I can tell you about Mel Renfro. He was *incredible*. It was like he knew where you were going. I can only say that he had that sense great defensive backs are born with. You just could not shake the guy. We'd scrimmage, and on most defenders I could plant that right foot and go, but I couldn't do that with Mel. He had this hip movement that allowed him to be right there with you no matter what cuts you made, no matter where you moved, no matter what you did. And he had the quickness of a jaguar or one of those cats that had speed *and* quickness, too. This was Mel Renfro, and he was amazing."

Lilly was also quoted in Golenbock's book on his teammate: "Finest cornerback I saw, with the exception of Mel Blount, during my years of watching football. They wouldn't throw at Renfro because he always intercepted it or knocked it down. Mel forced the other team to go all to the other side, and that way we could set up our defenses. Landry was able to create a situation where they had to throw over there, and we had some good cornerbacks, but unfortunately not another like Mel."

Teammate Charlie Waters supported Lilly's observation when quoted by the *Eugene Register-Guard* in 1996 on Renfro's play: "Mel would have had a lot more interceptions if I hadn't been playing the other corner. They threw at me every time. Poor Mel would have had 80 interceptions if he had as much activity as I had. His mere presence was awe-inspiring."

End Willie Townes 1966–67

Willie "Baby Cakes" Townes started his career as a defensive tackle when he was drafted by Dallas out of Tulsa. He was moved to defensive end in the middle of his rookie season and replaced Larry Stephens in the starting lineup.

Image provided by Steve Liskey - RetroCards.net

Willie Townes

"Willie was one of the big guys who was fined many times by Coach Tom Landry and relegated to the 'Fat Man's table,'" said Mel. "Coach wanted his linemen to be lean and mean. Speed and quickness were Townes' strength. He had the ability to evade blockers. A thigh injury and calcium deposits in the knees ended his career. He was fun and a party guy."

Townes recorded 15 sacks during his two seasons before he was replaced by rookie Larry Cole when he suffered knee problems. Townes was best known for causing Green Bay quarterback Bart Starr to fumble in the 1967 NFL championship "Ice Bowl" game.

End Larry Cole 1968–80

Larry "Bubba" Cole was drafted by Dallas in the 16th round out of Houston in the 1968 draft as an offensive tackle, but was switched to defensive end during training camp. "Larry was small for a defensive end," said Mel. "But he was very smart and good at the point of attack."

Image provided by Steve Liskey - RetroCards.net

Larry Cole

Cole was credited with a career total of 60 sacks in his 13-year career as a Cowboy. He played in five Super Bowls.

"He was the jokester of the defense," said Mel. "He always had something funny to say. I remember best Cole's comment explaining quarterback Clint Longley's debut win when he replaced an injured Roger Staubach: 'He mastered Landry's complicated system – a triumph of an uncluttered mind.'"

End George Andrie 1962–72

Image provided by
Steve Liskey - RetroCards.net

George Andrie

George Andrie came to Dallas as a sixth-round draft pick out of Marquette in 1962.

"He was one of the greatest defensive ends in Cowboys history," said Renfro. "George fit Coach Landry's defensive model. He was lean and mean. At 6-6, with long arms to bat down passes, George was an outstanding defensive end. He was a good technician, strong at the point of attack, predictable and positive. He let his play speak for him. He always did his job well and always graded high."

Andrie became a starter as a rookie and was a great pass rusher through his 11-year Cowboy career, recording 97 sacks.

In the Ice Bowl, Andrie picked up a fumble and ran it in for a touchdown. He was All-Pro in 1969 and a five-time Pro Bowl selection.

Tackle Jethro Pugh 1965–78

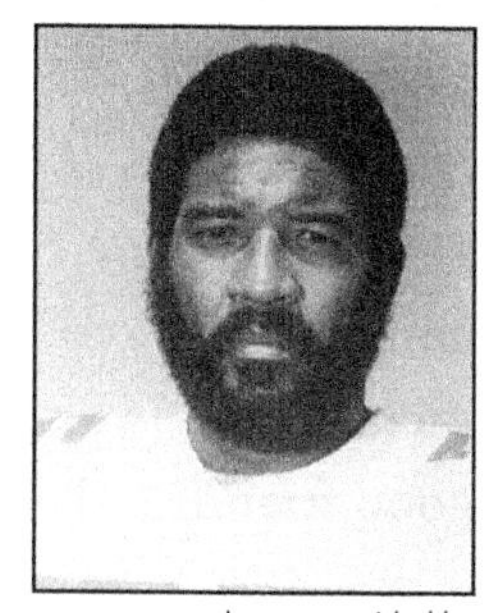

Image provided by
Steve Liskey - RetroCards.net

Jethro Pugh

Jethro Pugh – nicknamed "Buzz or Buzzard" – was drafted by the Cowboys as a 20-year-old in the 11th round in 1965 out of Elizabeth City State in North Carolina. In 1966, he replaced Jim Colvin in the starting lineup. At 6-6 and 260, Pugh was physical and athletic and became an excellent pass rusher. He recorded 95 ½ sacks during his 14-year Cowboy career.

Though he led the Doomsday Defense in sacks from 1968 to 1972, he was never voted to the Pro Bowl, often overshadowed by teammates Lilly and Andrie.

"Buzz was a big strong D-tackle, a good pass rusher," said Renfro. "He had nine unassisted tackles in one game. He was one of the teammates I enjoyed hanging with. He is a close friend to this day."

Tackle Bob Lilly 1961–74

Image provided by Steve Liskey - RetroCards.net

Bob Lilly

Bob Lilly, a consensus All-American from Texas Christian, was the Cowboys' first pick, 13th overall, in 1961. Lilly was available for the Cowboys that late in the draft because he let it be known he would only play pro football in his home state of Texas. Lilly began as a defensive end, but midway through his third season, Landry moved him to defensive tackle. Lilly became the main man in the Cowboys' Doomsday Defense.

As a tackle, Lilly was first team All-NFL every year from 1964 to 1969 and again in 1971. His 29-yard sack of Dolphin quarterback Bob Griese in Super Bowl VI is one of the most memorable plays in Super Bowl defensive history. *NFL Films'* feature on Lilly concluded he was "unblockable, unstoppable and the force of the Doomsday Defense." "Mr. Cowboy" played in 196 consecutive regular-season games over his 13 seasons.

"Lilly is one of the greatest defensive tackles to ever play the game," remarked Mel. "He was very quick off the ball and a sure tackler. Bob is one of the nicest guys I've ever known. We are still good friends today."

Linebacker Chuck Howley 1963–73

Chuck Howley – Renfro called him "Wanda," football-speak for weak-side linebacker – came to the Cowboys in a 1963 draft-day trade with the Chicago Bears as a gamble by Landry to strengthen his defense.

Image provided by Steve Liskey - RetroCards.net

Chuck Howley

"'Wanda' was big, athletic, fast, and tough. Nobody got by him," said Mel. "He was a terror. Sometimes I didn't know whether he was that good or just lucky. He played my side as the right outside linebacker and was prone to make mistakes in pass coverage. But if he did make a mistake, he usually made up for it with an interception."

Howley made All-Pro five times, played in six Pro Bowls and was the MVP of Super Bowl V.

Linebacker Dave Edwards 1963–75

"Fuzzy" was drafted by the AFL Denver Broncos out of Auburn in 1962. He opted to sign as a free agent with the Cowboys in 1963. Edwards started as a rookie when Howley was moved from strong-side to weak-side linebacker. It was decided that Edwards had more upper-body strength.

Image provided by Steve Liskey - RetroCards.net

Dave Edwards

"Fuzzy, or 'Sara' (strong-side linebacker) as I called him, was tough as nails," Renfro said. "Nobody got by him. He was a hard hitter who played extremely well against the run."

Middle Linebacker Lee Roy Jordan 1963–76

Lee Roy Jordan, a linebacker and center at Alabama, was the Cowboys' No. 1 draft pick in 1963. He replaced Jerry Tubbs as the club's starter.

Image provided by Steve Liskey - RetroCards.net

Lee Roy Jordon

"Although he was only 6-1 and 215 pounds, 'Meg' (middle linebacker) was a great competitor to play Coach Landry's flex defense with unmatched intensity," said Mel. "'Killer' (another Jordan nickname) was one of the best middle linebackers in the league. He plugged the middle of the line like a bulldozer. His favorite words were, 'Keep (the opponent) out of the (red) zone,' which he did well. He hurt people he was so intense. We all looked up to Lee Roy. He kept us going."

Jordan had a team-record of 21 tackles in a game against Philadelphia in 1971. In 14 NFL seasons, Jordan intercepted 32 passes, recovered 18 fumbles and made 743 solo tackles. He played in five Pro Bowls, was once an All-Pro selection and was the NFL's Defensive Player of the Year in 1973. Jordan teamed with Howley and Edwards to form one of the greatest linebacking corps in NFL history.

Cornerback/Safety Cornell Green 1962–74

Cornell Green, a 6-3, 205-pound All-American basketball player from Utah State, was an undrafted free agent with Dallas in 1962 who learned fast enough to start three games his rookie year. During his second season, he had seven interceptions.

Image provided by Steve Liskey - RetroCards.net

Cornell Green

Nicknamed "Sweet Lips" by teammate Bob Hayes, Green became a big-time contributor to Landry's intricate defensive schemes. He was a feared defender during his 13 seasons with the Cowboys, never missing a game. Green made five Pro Bowls at two different positions, cornerback and strong safety. He played corner his first eight seasons and was named NFL All-Pro four times. When Mike Gaechter ended his career in 1970, Landry moved Renfro to play corner and Green to strong safety to be matched up with Herb Adderley. After the switch, the Cowboys went to two consecutive Super Bowls.

"Cornell was as good as any cover corner in the league," said Mel. "I studied his techniques before I moved to corner. He had great foot movement and was a hard hitter. He was a friendly guy. Everyone got along well with Cornell."

Cornerback Herb Adderley 1970–72

Herb Adderley had a four-year All-Pro career with the Green Bay Packers (1961–1969) as a defensive back before he was traded in 1970 to the Cowboys for center Malcolm Walker and defensive end Clarence Williams. It happened after Adderley accused his head coach Phil Bengtson of keeping him off the Pro Bowl team the previous season.

Image provided by Steve Liskey - RetroCards.net

Herb Adderley

"Herb was emotionally tough," said Renfro. "He was a big influence on us going to Super Bowls V and VI. He brought that Green Bay toughness into the locker room. I remember in training camp after a 38-0 loss to the St. Louis Cardinals, when the guys were hanging their heads, he went off on us. All hell broke loose from inside a number 26 jersey. 'You guys are a miserable bunch of losers!' He got our attention. He brought the Lombardi quality of 'No crap, let's get it done.' He was very tough-minded. Herb and I were roommates the three years he was a Cowboy."

Safety Mike Gaechter 1962–69

Image provided by Steve Liskey - RetroCards.net

Mike Gaechter

It was an amazing story for Michael Gaechter, a football and track athlete at Oregon who became a first-time starter for the Ducks in his senior season. Gaechter parlayed a free-agent opportunity into an eight-season pro career as a strong safety for the Cowboys. In college, Gaechter was a teammate of Renfro in both sports.

"Mike had tremendous speed," said Mel. "With the Cowboys, we really got along well together. He was a real encouragement to me. He taught me a lot about how fast the pro game was, and that I should do all right with my skills."

Gaechter earned a reputation as a feared hitter in the Cowboy secondary, selling out his body for the sake of the team. In eight seasons he recorded 21 interceptions with the Cowboys. He ruptured his Achilles tendon in the 1969 NFL playoffs against the Rams, ending his career. He died in August 2015.

Safety Cliff Harris 1970–79

Image provided by Steve Liskey - RetroCards.net

Cliff Harris

Nicknamed "Captain Crash," Cliff Harris signed with Dallas as a free agent in 1970 out of Ouachita Baptist University, a NAIA school, and beat out third-round draft choice Charlie Waters for the free safety position his rookie year.

Harris changed the way the position was played. He played the pass well and struck fear into opponents because he hit so hard. He made five Super Bowl appearances, played in the Pro Bowl six times and was named All-Pro four times. Harris made the Cowboy Ring of Honor in 2004.

"Crash would hit anything that moved, even his own teammates," cracked Mel. "One game, I made a tackle and he hit me instead of the receiver."

Doomsday Coaches

Ernie Stautner 1966–88

The German-born Ernie Stautner played his entire pro football career with the Pittsburgh Steelers from 1950 to 1963. Even though he was small for a lineman at 6-1 and 235 pounds, he distinguished himself as one of the best defensive linemen of his era. From 1966 to 1988, he was defensive line coach with Dallas, becoming the defensive coordinator in 1973. The Doomsday Defense began to emerge after Stautner's arrival. His defenses helped the club win division titles from 1966 to 1970, but the team could not win a championship. Doomsday showed its greatness in 1971, dominating the Miami Dolphins in a 24-3 victory in Super Bowl VI. Stautner's Doomsday II would carry Dallas to its second Super Bowl title in 1977 with a 27-10 defeat of the Denver Broncos.

"Ernie instituted one missing ingredient for us – ferocity," said Renfro. "Until he arrived, we had been on our own. We worked hard, but you aren't going to accomplish much unless you have someone pushing you a little harder than you want to go, and we didn't have that. He made us much more aware of our jobs during the game. He put us up to another level."

Jerry Tubbs 1968–89

Jerry Tubbs watched the Cowboys grow into America's Team – first as a player for six years, as a player-coach for two years, then as a full-time linebacker coach in 1968 under Landry, a role he would fill for 21 years. During his time at Breckenridge (Texas) High and three years playing for Bud Wilkinson at Oklahoma, Tubbs never lost a game. Tubbs coached in five Super Bowls with Dallas, winning two. "The only reason we got him was because he told the 49ers he was going to retire," said vice president/player personnel Gil Brandt. Tubbs shared many of the same personality traits that Landry had. An analytical type, he was more reserved than vocal. "Tom had a great deal of faith in him as a coach," Brandt said. "Jerry was very smart, and he was one of the toughest guys." Tubbs died in 2012 at 77.

"Tubbs handled the transition to coaching very well," recalled Renfro. "He was nuts and bolts. Everybody loved him."

Bobby Ray Franklin 1968–72

Bobby Ray Franklin, Sugar Bowl MVP for Mississippi in 1960, played for the Cleveland Browns from 1960 to 1966. He was hired by the Cowboys as defensive backfield and special teams coach from 1968 to 1972 after two seasons coaching at Georgia Tech. He coached in Super Bowls V and VI. Franklin was the head coach at Northwest CC in Mississippi from 1981 to 2005, enjoying 25 consecutive winning seasons.

"Bobby was a really nice coach, always happy," said Mel. "He was blessed by having good players. He enjoyed going through the drills. We loved him! He was comfortable for us to work with."

Dick Nolan 1962–66

A former New York Giant teammate of Landry, Dick Nolan played nine seasons in the NFL as a defensive back, mostly with the Giants. He came to Dallas as a player-coach in 1962. Nolan played cornerback until he was injured halfway through his first season; then he took over the defensive coaching duties. "Landry let me run the defense while he ran the offense," reported Nolan at the time. "He never bothered me at all." After five seasons with the Cowboys, Nolan's first head-coaching job covered eight seasons (1968–75) with the San Francisco 49ers, and he served the same capacity with the New

Orleans Saints from 1978 to 1980. "Everything I know from football I learned from Tom Landry," Nolan told Red Smith of *The New York Times* in 1972. He led the 49ers to three consecutive NFC Western Division titles. In the two conference championship games, his 49ers lost to Landry's Cowboys. His 1970 team, with John Brodie at quarterback, finished with a 10-3-1 record and led the league in offense; Nolan was named the NFL coach of the year. He was fired after the Saints started the 1980 season 0-12. Nolan served as defensive coordinator for the Houston Oilers in 1981 before he returned to be a Cowboy assistant (1982–90). Nolan suffered from Alzheimer's disease and prostate cancer before he died at 75 in 2007.

"Dick was a very knowledgeable coach and a good communicator," said Renfro. "I loved playing for him."

Gene Stallings 1972–85

Gene Stallings played end at Texas A&M under Bear Bryant as a member of the famed "Junction Boys" in 1956, who finished 9-0-1 to capture their first Southwest Conference championship. After a stint of seven years on Bryant's original staff at Alabama (the Crimson Tide won national championships in 1961 and 1964), Stallings was head coach at Texas A&M for seven seasons. In 1972, he joined the Dallas staff as Landry's secondary coach. He remained for 14 years and helped the Cowboys win Super Bowl XII. From 1986 to 1989, Stallings was head coach of the St. Louis/Phoenix Cardinals. He resigned in 1989 to become the head coach at Alabama, where he went 62-25 before retiring in 1996. His 1992 team won the National Championship.

Landry added a defensive back coach to his staff for the first time in 1972 when he hired Stallings. He became Mel's defensive back coach for six years. Stallings got his first taste of professional football players when he tried to institute a tackling drill for the defensive backs. Mel interrupted him early: "We don't tackle in practice."

"At first when Stallings came," cornerback Claxton Welch said, "Mel would coach while Coach Stallings would stand on the sidelines and learn as Mel took over the practice."

"Gene spent the first two years learning Landry's pro football system," said Mel, "always studying, watching and repeating for his own benefit. Then in his third year, he brought into the program some of his own defenses that were effective. He loved his players, and he was truly family-oriented."

20

Disappointment

1972	(11-5-0)		
S17	Eagles	W	28-6
S24	@Giants	W	23-14
O1	@Packers	L	13-16
O8	Steelers	W	17-13
O15	@Colts	W	21-0
O22	@Redskins	L	20-24
O30	Lions	W	28-24
N5	@Chargers	W	34-28
N12	Cardinals	W	33-24
N19	@Eagles	W	28-7
N23	49ers	L	10-31
D3	@Cardinals	W	27-6
D9	Redskins	W	34-24
D17	Giants	L	3-23
	Playoffs		
D23	@49ers	W	30-28
D31	@Redskins	L	3-26

In 1972, Richard Nixon was still in office, causing heated debates between the liberal players and the conservatives in the NFL.

Many who were anti-war spoke out loudly against the Nixon regime, the war and racism. All were disappointed when Nixon defeated Democratic candidate George McGovern. Roger Staubach had been to Vietnam, and he continued to strongly defend America's right to be there, but the quarterback surprised some of his teammates by siding with the blacks on the racial issue. He spoke up and supported them, earning gratitude and increased respect from his black teammates.

"America's Team"

The Cowboys appeared so often on TV, Bob Ryan of *NFL Films* called them "America's Team." They became the most popular team in the country. The name stuck. The cowboy image – they were America itself. Cowboys, the real kind, saddle ponies, lariats, and 10-gallon hats have always been bigger than life for America.

The Cowboys introduced their new creation, the Dallas Cowboy Cheerleaders, wearing star-spangled uniforms and performing dance routines instead of acrobatic displays. The football team wore their white uniforms all season.

The Adderley Saga

With Herb Adderley serving as co-captain, the Cowboys overcame the off-field squabble and won Super Bowl VI in convincing fashion. The Doomsday Defense came of age and completely stopped Miami 24-3.

Safety Cornell Green said it was Adderley who pushed Dallas over the top while defensive back Mark Washington also agreed. "If Herb hadn't come to us when he did, we don't go to any Super Bowls, period," said Washington. "That's the kind of effect he had on the team; there was nobody on the team who was more positive."

According to defensive end Pat Toomay, Landry spent the off-season fixating on the win. For an ultra-control person, believing Adderley was the reason the Cowboys won it all in 1971 implied it really wasn't his. It meant he couldn't win the crown without a Vince Lombardi player.

When training camp started the next season, Tom Landry went on a personal vendetta against Adderley. He wanted control. He immediately demoted Adderley as the team co-captain and proceeded to challenge his preseason conditioning. By the end of the eight games, Landry tested his obedience by forcing a confrontation at a team film session of the previous game. He criticized Adderley's playing technique for not following the Flex's defensive "keys." As the reviewed play was under way, Herb instinctively reacted when the ball was in the air and knocked down a sure touchdown pass. But it didn't impress his coach: Herb was accused of not following his keys, but guessing.

Adderley reacted and rose to defend himself. "It was an unprecedented moment for the team," said Toomay. "No player had ever challenged the coach." Adderley paid the price of disobedience. He was benched for the season and was replaced by Charley Waters.

"We knew never to question Landry," said Mel Renfro. "Whether we knew he was right or wrong, we never questioned it; we just accepted it. Herb questioned him right there in the meeting. Landry got real tense and things just didn't seem to be the same after that. Landry put Herb on the bench and put Waters in there, which in everybody's opinion was a big mistake."

As a side note, years later Renfro, the top defensive back to play for Landry, weighed in regarding the Flex for Jeff Sullivan's *America's Team* production: "The only thing I understand about the Flex was that the front seven would line up in funny positions. I have absolutely no clue to this day what the defensive line and linebackers were doing with the Flex. Luckily, it didn't apply to the defensive backs."

The 1972 Season

Before the season started, Craig Morton – not wanting sit on the bench again – asked Landry for the opportunity to win the starting quarterback job back. But Coach Tom Landry made up his mind that Staubach was going to be his quarterback.

The defending Super Bowl champions had high expectations for the year. But things changed in the third exhibition game against the Rams. As Staubach was cutting back on a scramble, linebacker Marlin McKeever separated the quarterback's shoulder with a vicious hit. The 1972 campaign hadn't even started and the Cowboys were facing the season without their two top stars, the traded Duane Thomas and Roger Staubach out for 8–12 weeks.

Morton got his quarterback job back and Calvin Hill, who spent two years of frustration nursing injuries and playing behind Thomas, returned as a starter.

Morton had a good season. With his leadership and passing, the offense was consistent, executing Landry's game plans. With a big boost from the Doomsday II Defense, the Cowboys finished the regular season 10-4. Hill finished with 1,036 yards rushing, but Bob Hayes didn't catch a touchdown pass all season. Newcomer Lance Alworth of Charger fame and Ron Sellers picked up the slack in the receiving department.

The Cowboys lost their stranglehold on the NFC East title by losing to the New York Giants in the regular-season finale 23-3, but still earned a wild card playoff berth to face the San Francisco 49ers.

The playoff game with the 49ers was crazy. After San Francisco's Vic Washington returned the opening kickoff 97 yards for a TD, Morton had a fumble and an interception that led to a three-score deficit. With Dallas trailing 28-13 at the end of the third quarter, 49er linebacker Dave Wilcox began to hassle the Cowboy offense: "How does it feel to be losing the big one?"

Morton launched a 50-yarder to Hayes, who couldn't hold onto it in the end zone. Then the stoic and focused Landry lost his cool. In an act of desperation, he benched Morton and inserted the rehabilitated Staubach, who had seen limited action during the regular season, completing 9 of 20 passes for 98 yards.

Staubach engineered a long drive and a field goal, bringing the game within two scores. Then, end Billy Parks caught Staubach's post pass for a touchdown with a minute and half left to close the gap to 28-23. The Cowboys still had an opportunity for an onside kick, and Mel Renfro, who always played on the kickoff team, was there to recover it.

"Toni Fritsch, the Austrian soccer player, caught everyone by surprise," remembered Mel. "We thought it was going to the left when he whirled around and kicked the ball with his left foot to the right. I saw it bounce off one of the San Francisco players and I just dove on it."

Actually, 49er Preston Riley grabbed for the unexpected ball and was hit by Cowboy rookie Ralph Coleman, popping the ball loose.

Staubach faked a pass and ran for 21 yards, then hit Parks again for 19. From the San Francisco 10, there was still time on the clock when Landry sent in a pass play for Billy Parks. But in the huddle, Ron Sellers, who had led the Cowboys with 31 receptions during the regular season, mentioned to the future "Captain Comeback," "I can get open."

Staubach found Sellers in the end zone for the touchdown to give Dallas an improbable 30-28 win. "It was one of the most exciting and remarkable endings to a football game I've ever seen," remarked Landry.

It was a devastating loss for the 49ers, who had beaten the

Cowboys 31-10 in November. Wilcox, Mel's teammate at Oregon and a future Pro Hall of Famer, threw his helmet 50 feet in the air in disgust. "Losing that game to the Cowboys just killed us," San Francisco coach Dick Nolan said. "That was the third year in a row we lost to the Cowboys."

The Disappointing Loss

Since Morton had always played well against the Washington Redskins during the 10-win regular season and the Cowboy offense was more accustomed to playing for him, many of the players wanted Morton to start in the NFC Championship game. But Landry stayed with Staubach, hoping his magic would continue similar to the victory over the 49ers. It didn't happen.

Renfro remembered vividly how disappointed he was during the week of practice before the Redskin game. "I couldn't understand where Landry was coming from," he said. "He approached the week critical of everyone's play in the previous game, instead of praising and encouraging the guys. It was **not** a good week of practice."

In his book *Lombardi's Left Side*, Adderley made an argument that Landry's coaching decisions cost his team a shot to play in three straight Super Bowls. During the playoff game at Washington, receiver Charley Taylor was having a strong game before defensive back Charley Waters broke his arm early in the fourth quarter when the Redskins led just 10-3.

"When Waters broke his arm, I ran on the field to replace him," Adderley said. "Landry yelled at me, 'Come off the field' and he yelled for Mark Washington to replace Waters."

On the Redskin sideline, their coach George Allen licked his chops when he recognized how Landry was shuffling his defense. He called timeout and brought his quarterback Billy Kilmer and Taylor over to call pass plays to be thrown at Washington. The second play of the fourth quarter Kilmer connected with Taylor with a perfectly thrown fly-route turnout for a 45-yard touchdown pass – it extended their lead to 17-3 and broke the Cowboys' spirit. The Redskins connected on three additional field goals to finish the game.

Even the victimized Washington, who was coming off a leg injury, weighed in on the event. "I thought Herb was going in, he was the backup; I was coming off an injury and I wasn't even warmed up. I didn't know what was going on. I had been practicing on the right side, not the left."

Taylor admitted that he and the Redskins benefitted from Landry's decision. "If Herb would have been in there, it would have been a **whole** different story."

The Cowboys struggled to execute Landry's four-wide-receiver-game plan designed specifically for the game. Roger Staubach was 9-20 for 98 yards and rushed for 59 yards on five carries to lead the Cowboy offense. The Redskins won 26-3 with Kilmer's two long touchdown passes to Taylor the key plays. It was the Skins' day.

The disappointed Cowboys finished 11-5. Miami, the team they had beaten the previous Super Bowl, defeated the Redskins 14-7 in the Los Angeles Coliseum in Super Bowl VII, becoming the first team to finish with an undefeated season.

Renfro earned his ninth Pro Bowl selection. The 23rd Pro Bowl was played at Texas Stadium, where Tom Landry's NFC team lost to Chuck Noll's AFC team 33-28. O.J. Simpson was the MVP. The winning AFC players received $2,000 apiece, while the losers each took home $1,500.

The 1973 Season

1973	(11-5-0)		
S16	@Bears	W	20-17
S24	Saints	W	40-3

1973	(11-5-0)		
S30	Cardinals	W	45-10
O8	@Redskins	L	7-14
O14	@Rams	L	31-37
O21	Giants	W	45-28
O28	@Eagles	L	16-30
N4	Bengals	W	38-10
N11	@Giants	W	23-10
N18	Eagles	W	31-10
N22	Dolphins	L	7-14
D2	@Broncos	W	22-10
D9	Redskins	W	27-7
D16	@Cardinals	W	30-3
	Playoffs		
D23	Rams	W	27-16
D30	Vikings	L	10-27

Staff and Player Uncertainty

Landry always re-evaluated the prior season and usually decided on a recommitment to excellence – a tougher and more demanding approach. But at the start of the 1973 season, many members of the coaching staff – Bobby Franklin, Ray Renfro (no relation to Mel), Sid Gillman and Dan Reeves – left for other jobs.

Reeves was unhappy because Landry let Gillman run the offense, and in Landry's autobiography, the coach said he refused to recommend Reeves for the head coaching position at Southern Methodist, telling him he was "too young." Reeves left football entirely for a year and went into real estate. In July, Ermal Allen, the offensive coach, had a heart attack and had to be replaced.

There were also player departures. Tight end Mike Ditka and

linebacker Chuck Howley retired; cornerback Herb Adderley was traded first to New England, then to the Rams, but retired instead; unhappy receiver Lance Alworth was disappointed with the "uninspired" passing game and quit; and defensive end George Andrie left with back problems. Receiver Ron Sellers was traded to the Dolphins in exchange for the fast Otto Stowe, who was unhappy sitting while Paul Warfield played.

Then there were problems with salaries of Dallas's unhappy top players. They were frustrated with president/general manager Tex Schramm's stubborn stinginess and went to the media with their unhappiness. Renfro, Morton, Bob Lilly and Jordan led the charge.

Mel was upset with the Cowboy tactics, especially with how Schramm wanted to control the players with an iron hand, which included their salaries. Dallas didn't keep up with the marketplace in the NFL. When Mel's salary was at the $35,000-a-year level, his counterpart safety Larry Wilson of the St. Louis Cardinals was being paid $100,000 – nearly three times what the Cowboys were willing to pay Renfro.

Morton was bitter about not starting in the 1972 NFC Championship game. If he had to sit behind Staubach, Morton would be penalized twice because of incentive clauses in his contract. He walked out of training camp in mid-July, asking to be traded.

With Morton absent from camp for more than a week, Staubach was assured by his coach he would be the starter. Center Dave Manders was refused a no-trade clause and held out during the exhibition season. He was found to be irreplaceable and returned when the season started.

The only player to win big over Schramm was Jordan. He was offered $50,000 during a season in which the Bears' Dick Butkus was making $150,000. Jordan didn't walk out until the last linebacker cuts were made, leaving Landry with only a rookie to replace him.

Landry was upset. Then Schramm, who didn't like to be

outsmarted, made a $100,000 offer, but the encounter initially kept Jordan from being named to the Cowboy Ring of Honor. Jordan was honored in 1989, only after Schramm was dismissed in 1988.

The draft included tight end Billy Joe DuPree, wide receiver Golden Richards, defensive end Harvey Martin, tackle Bruce Walton and linebacker Rodrigo Barnes. Jim Meyers took over as the offensive coordinator.

The Free Agent – Drew Pearson

Drew Pearson, a quarterback at Tulsa, signed as a free agent with the Cowboys for a $150 bonus. He was listed as the No. 8 receiver during the February rookie minicamp. Those who excelled at the camp were invited the following month to the veterans' minicamp. "That was an inspiration to me to really get after it to make the team," said Pearson.

As the spring went on, Pearson moved to Dallas near the practice facility, took a warehouse job for $7 an hour and began working out in preparation for the 1973 training camp. Until that time, no one had worked as hard as Staubach. That changed when Pearson arrived. Day after day, it would be two workaholics – the famous quarterback and the unknown rookie free agent – running pass pattern after pass pattern. The skinny kid from New Jersey, as Peter Golenbock noted in his book *Landry's Boys,* "had great desire, good speed and great hands as well."

Staubach gained confidence in Pearson as a receiver. When he got a chance in a game, he made plays, a pass catch or block or whatever. He continued to make plays, and ended up on the roster.

"Drew was real spunky," said Renfro. "He was real confident in his ability. He developed a good rhythm with his work ethic. He wore this big Afro and he was real funny. He kept us laughing all the time. He and Roger would concoct these plays to beat me in practice, but he could never beat me."

Quarterback Controversy

As 1972 was Morton's year to shine and lead the Cowboys to the division championship while an injured Staubach rehabbed, 1973 was Staubach's season to lead the team to the division crown. The difference was that Craig was physically well and was in top form in preseason. That concerned Roger, because he never knew what his coach was thinking.

Staubach forced the issue. He went to Landry and told his coach he needed to make a decision and stick to it, and if he wasn't the starter in 1973, he wanted to be traded to Atlanta. Landry assured him, "You're going to be my quarterback."

In 1973, Staubach led the NFL in passing with 2,428 yards while running for another 250 yards. Hill ran for 1,142 yards and led the team in receptions with 32 catches for 290 yards.

The debate that season was in the receiving corps. It was evident the Cowboys were force-feeding Golden Richards while demoting Hayes. Landry's confidence in Hayes was so low that Hayes asked to be traded. It caused disharmony.

When injuries took their toll on receivers, the free-agent rookie got his chance. Pearson played his first season and became one of the greatest receivers in Cowboys history.

Landry gradually worked Pearson into the lineup, and in the Thanksgiving Day loss to the Dolphins, the skinny receiver ended up catching eight passes – all on inside routes while turning and making tough-catch plays.

In the division playoff game with the Rams, the quarterback-receiver combo improvised a pass play. With Dallas ahead 17-16,

Landry ordered a sideline pass to Hayes, but Staubach told Pearson to change his turn-in route to a post pattern.

After Staubach asked for maximum protection, Pearson took off on the post and was double- covered by Eddie McMillan and Steve Preece. "No way should he have thrown it, but here it came," remembered Pearson. "I caught the ball between the corner and the safety before they ran into each other, and I was gone for an 83-yard touchdown."

Ram safety Preece remembered the play differently.

"I anticipated Staubach's deep pass to Pearson," said Preece. "I shaded away from Pearson's side, knowing that an interception would put us back into the game. I intercepted the ball over the top, but had a collision with Eddie Mac, popping the football loose."

The ball landed on Pearson's hip. A picture in the *LA Times* labeled "Drew stole Xmas" showed Pearson with his eyes closed and hands at his waist before he responded with his catch. The Cowboys won 27-16.

NFC Championship Loss

The Cowboys earned their fourth straight NFC Championship Game appearance. However, not even the home crowd at Texas Stadium could help them as they fell to the Minnesota Vikings 27-10 with a trip to the Super Bowl on the line.

"Minnesota quarterback Fran Tarkenton was the toughest player to play against," Renfro said. "We couldn't catch him. A running quarterback wearing us down became a problem. He scrambled all day long."

Tenth Pro Bowl

Mel played in his 10th consecutive and final Pro Bowl January 20, 1974, at Arrowhead Stadium in Kansas City. The NFC was coached by Landry against the AFC's John Madden. Kicker Garo Yepremian earned the MVP honors with five field goals in the AFL's 15-13 win.

Mel earned 1st team All-NFC and All-NFL honors from the Associated Press, *Pro Football Weekly*, *Sporting News*, and UPI.

21

1974 and the Move to Portland

In 1972, after a year living during the offseason in Thousand Oaks, California, the Renfros became homesick. They made the decision to move back to Portland to put down roots, build a family home and invest $30,000 in a family business venture. They chose Wood Village, a suburban neighborhood on the northeast outskirts of Portland, and started their kids – Melvin, 8, Tony, 7, and Cynthia, 4 – in the Reynolds School District.

Cowboy teammates Les Shy and Dickie Daniels introduced Los Angeles agent Chuck Dekeado to Mel. It set the stage for Mel's business relationship with him, and they became good friends. At the time, General Manager Tex Schramm would not allow agents to negotiate Cowboy contracts. Since he helped Shy open "Les Shy's Bicycle City" in LA, Mel utilized Dekeado for his Portland start-up.

In 1974, with the help of Dekeado and fellow NFL player and realtor Steve Preece, Mel rented a strip-mall building on Portland's Southeast Powell to open Mel Renfro's Bicycle City, which featured imported bikes. It was managed by his brother James.

The second investment, Renfro's Carpet Cleaning business, had a small warehouse on Northeast Cully. It was managed by his brother Dallas and wife Rhodella. Dallas did the job bidding while their dad, Dallas Sr., and brother Raye did the carpet cleaning.

The start-ups struggled financially. After a year, Mel had to close both of his operations down. They weren't profitable for their absentee owner. "The economy was bad for opening a bike shop, and the bids for the carpet cleaning business were too low to make a profit," said Mel.

Mel wasn't business-savvy. His college experience at Oregon only allowed him to develop and showcase his athletic talent well enough to be drafted and play professional football. That was a huge accomplishment, but it didn't prepare him for the business world. As a married, two-sport minority athlete without a strong scholastic background, Mel shorted himself on education. With year-round time constraints on a two-sport athlete, he had struggled just to stay eligible at Oregon.

Renfro's lack of understanding the consequences of poor business decisions plagued him throughout his career. Listening to the locker-room gossip of his teammates extolling their off-season jobs and investments didn't help him, either. What Mel needed was a successful business person to advise him, a relationship-type person whom he could learn to trust – not a salesman or a sports agent.

Another person took notice of Renfro. Irv Cross, a former Eagle and Ram cornerback who became the first African-American analyst and commentator for CBS Sports in 1971, had a McDonald's franchise for Renfro to consider. "But his agent tracked him to a bicycle store in Portland," recalled Cross. "Mel had a penchant for bad business decisions. It was unfortunate."

Renfro also had a penchant for beer. From Mel's accident following JFK's assassination, when his slashed wrist ended his collegiate career, to his week-long binge following Dr. Martin Luther

King's death, this personal weakness was exposed: Mel had a serious drinking problem. Its consequences would affect his marriage, his family and his future.

Car Accidents

To compound issues in his life in the spring of 1974, Mel had two drunk-driving accidents.

"I was hanging out, doing a little drinking late at night, and ran off the road on my way home," recalled Mel. "I hit a ditch and flipped the car upside down, totaling the car. I walked home.

"The second accident two months later, I wasn't as fortunate. I was only half a mile from home when I hit a guy on his way to work – it was at slow speed but head-on. I ended up with a stiff neck, but neither of us were hurt although I totaled my second car."

The second accident forced Mel into some decision making. "I told myself, 'I've got to sober up,'" he said.

Mel literally took flight. He immediately returned to Dallas without his family.

"To sober up, I went back to Dallas, checked into a motel behind the practice facility and stayed in my room for a week or two before I was able to even work out," he said. "In four or five weeks, I was back in good shape. Then I rented an apartment and decided to stay in Dallas permanently. I never went back to Portland except for visits."

There was a heartfelt sadness for Mel, who missed his kids. "It was tough," he said. "I didn't see my children."

Mel admitted his drinking behavior was the breaking point of his marriage.

"While living apart those three years, Pat refused to come to Dallas for any of my games," he said. "She didn't want to be married anymore."

After 15 years of marriage, Pat and Mel divorced in 1976. It came at a time Mel was at the peak of his career, earning an $80,000 salary with the Cowboys – his next to last year as a player. The timing of an alimony settlement of $1,500 a month became an unfortunate problem for Mel. Within a year, Mel was to take an 86 percent reduction in income, making but $1,000 a month as a Cowboy scout for Gil Brandt.

The financial squeeze would cause Mel great stress, trouble in court and embarrassment. It came at a time in his life when he didn't have a plan for life after football.

Pat and the kids remained in Portland. She downsized their home and gained a job as a fingerprint specialist and secretary with the Portland Police Department, a position in which she served for over 30 years.

Mel on Drinking

When Mel was questioned about his beer-drinking problem, he answered frankly: "I usually have a few beers in the evening. The times when I had too much were the times I was depressed or angry and I got off to myself. I've been able to deal with it later in my life without help and without intervention."

Mel on Drugs and Marijuana

"I never knew drugs, but I had tried marijuana once or twice. I sat in a session or two with that stuff and it about killed me. So that was the end of that. I couldn't handle it."

The World Football League

The Cowboys' 1974 season was marked by tension and division. The World Football League came into existence, causing Schramm difficulty in his salary negotiations.

The general manager's hard line policy of paying the players half the going rate was in trouble. Suddenly, the players had another avenue to take. Schramm learned he had to pay the going rate to secure Ed "Too Tall" Jones, their first-round pick. He signed a three-year, $400,000 contract, about twice what he would have been offered if it weren't for the WFL's Detroit Wheels. Third-round draft pick Danny White, a quarterback out of Arizona State, signed with the WFL's Toronto Northmen, with an offer twice what Schramm wanted to pay him.

The Players' Strike

In addition to the Cowboys' battle to keep players from jumping to the other league, the NFL Players Association (NFLPA) went on strike July 1 over the free-agency issue. When training camp opened, the veterans refused to report, causing turmoil within the team. Many of the black players felt disrespected by their coach and the Cowboy organization. A lot of comments that were made stirred up animosity.

"The players who spoke up against the white players who opposed the strike for the most part were the young bucks who were into the power thing," said Renfro. "I don't want to say black power, but stand-up-for-your-rights power, and those are rights that will help minority players."

The NFLPA strike ended August 12. Landry extended the training camp two weeks. He worked the players hard. The rough terrain the players ran was called the "Ho Chi Minh Trail."

The 1974 Season

Quarterback Craig Morton demanded to be traded. The 10-year veteran was dealt to the New York Giants for a first-round draft pick and left with barely a thank you. Receiver Otto Stowe was pushed out when he complained of an ankle problem. He was traded to Denver for a draft pick. In October, Rodrigo Barnes, the outspoken linebacker who wanted Jordan's job, quit, then was traded in November to the Patriots.

The backup quarterback behind starter Roger Staubach now was Clint Longley, who had a good arm but lacked discipline. He had little interest in learning the keys of the Landry offense. He typically wanted to throw long and it drove Landry crazy.

1974	(8-6-0)		
S15	@Falcons	W	24-0
S23	@Eagles	L	10-13
S29	Giants	L	6-14
O6	Vikings	L	21-23
O13	@Cardinals	L	28-31
O20	Eagles	W	31-24
O27	@Giants	W	21-7
N3	Cardinals	W	17-14
N10	49ers	W	20-14
N17	@Redskins	L	21-28
N24	@Oilers	W	10-0
N28	Redskins	W	24-23
D7	Browns	W	41-17
D14	@Raiders	L	23-27

The season didn't start well. After shutting out the Falcons 24-0, the Cowboys lost four close games in a row by a total of 16 points. They closed the season by winning seven of the last nine games to finish with an 8-6 record.

The highlight of the season came on Thanksgiving Day when Longley led the Cowboys with a comeback win over the Washington Redskins. Trailing 16-3 in the second half, with Staubach out due to injury, the seldom used backup Longley threw two touchdowns to lead the team to a 24-23 victory at Texas Stadium.

Though the Cowboys were playing as well as any team in the league by season's end, their streak of eight straight seasons in the playoffs ended.

Staubach still put up good numbers, passing for 2,552 yards while rushing for an additional 320. Calvin Hill was below par for him, but earned another Pro Bowl season, gaining 844 yards on the ground. Billy Joe DuPree and Golden Richards had good seasons, although together they couldn't match Drew Pearson's first All-Pro season output. Pearson gained 1,087 yards on 62 catches.

22

Improbable Super Bowl X

1975	(12-5-0)		
S21	Rams	W	18-7
S28	Cardinals	W	37-31
O6	@Lions	W	36-10
O12	@Giants	W	13-7
O19	Packers	L	17-19
O26	@Eagles	W	20-17
N2	@Redskins	L	24-30
N10	Chiefs	L	31-34
N16	@Patriots	W	34-31
N23	Eagles	W	27-17
N30	Giants	W	14-3
D7	@Cardinals	L	17-31
D13	Redskins	W	31-10
D21	@Jets	W	31-21
	Playoffs		
D28	@Vikings	W	17-14
J4	@Rams	W	37-7
	Super Bowl X		
J18	Steelers	L	17-21

During the spring of 1975, Mel Renfro was feeling physically strong after working out at the Cowboys' facility regularly.

"I was in the best shape of my career," said Mel. "I was lifting weights and running, building up my muscles and strength, while losing 10 pounds. I played well that season. I graded out 'excellent' in every game. I don't know why I didn't make the Pro Bowl again. When we brought in the young guys – Preston Pearson, Randy White, Ed Jones and Tom Henderson – I knew we were a talented football team."

In the spring of '75, the NFLPA sued team owners in federal court in an attempt to gain free agency for the players. To succeed, the "Rozelle Rule" had to be overturned. By existing NFL rules, if a team signed another's free agent player, Commissioner Pete Rozelle would determine proper compensation.

Bob Hayes testified in court. During the offseason, the veteran receiver was interested in signing with Washington, but the Redskins decided against it, worried that Rozelle would give Dallas their star receiver Charley Taylor in compensation. The Miami Dolphins also wanted Hayes, but were afraid Rozelle's compensation would be their star, Paul Warfield.

In June 1975, veteran running back Walt Garrison suffered a career-ending leg injury in a rodeo competition in Bozeman, Montana, which was the bad news for the Cowboys. The good news was that the World Football League was suffering financial problems and its future seemed shaky.

D.D. Lewis's deal with the Memphis Southmen fell through and the linebacker returned to the Cowboys. This was offset by the announced retirements of three outstanding veterans – center Dave Manders, cornerback Cornell Green and defensive tackle Bob Lilly. Lilly received huge adulation from the media and his coach. "Bob Lilly was the best lineman I ever saw," said Tom Landry.

By July, with receiver Bob Hayes being traded to the San Francisco 49ers and running back Calvin Hill moving to Hawaii in the WFL, the criticism of Coach Tom Landry and General Manager

Tex Schramm by the black players quieted considerably, and peace returned to the Cowboys.

Renfro loved Hayes as a teammate.

"We were very good friends," Renfro said. "Bob was a good guy. We used to go at each other a lot in practice over the years. Against him, I would line up a lot deeper and read the quarterback's eyes."

Bob Hayes' departure was similar to Craig Morton's in 1973. They both played for the Cowboys for 10 seasons and left without fanfare. Hayes had revolutionized the game with his blazing speed, catching 365 passes for 7,295 yards and 71 touchdowns as a Cowboy. To this day, Hayes holds 10 regular-season receiving records, four punt return records and 22 overall franchise marks, making him one of the greatest to ever play for the Cowboys. Hayes played the 1975 season with the 49ers. He was honored with induction to the Cowboy Ring of Honor in September 23, 2001, before his death, at age 59, in 2002. He was inducted into the Pro Football Hall of Fame in 2009.

The "Dirty Dozen" Draft

Rd	1975 Draftee	Pos	College
1	Randy White	DT	Maryland
1	Thomas Henderson	LB	Langston
2	Burton Lawless	G	Florida
3	Bob Breunig	LB	Arizona State
4	Pat Donovan	T	Stanford
4	Randy Hughes	DB	Oklahoma
5	Kyle Davis	C	Oklahoma
6	Rolley Woolsey	DB	Boise State
7	Mike Hegman	LB	Tennessee St
9	Ed Jones	DB	Rutgers
13	Herbert Scott	G	Virginia Union
14	Scott Laidlaw	RB	Stanford

If the Cowboys were to improve, they needed to count upon their draft choices. From the Craig Morton trade to the New York Giants, the Cowboys received the No. 2 pick in the draft. They selected Maryland defensive end Randy White, a future Pro Hall of Famer. With their own first-round pick, they selected a small-college defensive standout, linebacker Thomas "Hollywood" Henderson from Langston, an all-black college in Oklahoma. Henderson began his college career as a walk-on and became an NAIA All-American. Henderson let it be known immediately that he was after D.D. Lewis's linebacker job.

Landry's coaching philosophy was tested in 1975. Landry always felt that rookies weren't prepared to absorb the system, execute his schemes and play at a level he demanded. A rookie usually needed to be in the system for a year to play for the Cowboys. As rookies, Landry's "Dirty Dozen" would have played behind such as Dave Manders, Cornell Green, Bob Hayes, Walt Garrison, Calvin Hill and Pat Toomay, the latter traded to Buffalo – had those veterans still been around.

Landry had little optimism for the season. Because he didn't have his usual high goals, he eased off his coaching intensity. By blending the rookies with the remaining regulars, the team came together. Led by the brash and talented Henderson, an enthusiasm developed throughout. The young players got better game by game.

Preston Pearson, a good receiver out of the backfield, was picked up on waivers from the Steelers. He was a useful addition for the Cowboys, taking some pressure off of Drew Pearson.

In the season opener, the Cowboys held the Rams to a lone touchdown in an 18-7 win. Lee Roy Jordan and Roger Staubach became encouraged. Everyone tried a little harder, scratching and making plays. It was arguably Landry's best season of coaching in his long career.

All the games were hard-fought battles. If the Cowboys lost a close one, they would bounce back and win the next two. When the

Cowboys were 7-3, Jordan made a short, memorable pep talk, challenging every player to play hard with the playoffs in mind.

Landry's gang of old vets and young kids secured a wild-card berth in the playoffs with a 10-4 record. It was a fun year for Renfro.

A "Hail Mary" Win over the Vikings

The 12-2 Minnesota Vikings were clear favorites to beat Dallas in the wild-card game. Fran Tarkenton was the No. 1 quarterback in the NFL and Chuck Foreman was one of the top backs in the league.

It was a tight, low-scoring game that took a classic Staubach "Hail Mary" to win. With the Vikings leading 14-10 and 1:51 left in the game, the Cowboys were stymied on their own 25- yard line with a fourth-and-16 situation. Then Drew Pearson, with no receptions the whole game, caught a pass on the sidelines for 22 yards and a first down.

A Staubach pass to Preston Pearson was dropped with 26 seconds to go. Staubach resorted to a successful pass route that had previously been made in a game against the Redskins. Drew Pearson went on a deep "in" route against cornerback Nate Wright, while Staubach looked off safety Paul Krause. The pass was underthrown and Pearson came over the top of Wright to make the catch. Wright fell on the ground and Pearson took the ball into the end zone for the touchdown.

The Cowboys emerged with a 17-14 victory, causing a euphoric reaction on the Dallas sidelines and back in the city of Dallas.

NFC Championship Upset of the Rams

The underdog Cowboys came into the Los Angeles Coliseum before 88,919 and dominated the Los Angeles Rams for the NFC Championship, winning 37-7. Staubach passed for 220 yards and four touchdowns while rushing for 54 yards. The Cowboys played with a high level of confidence, while the Doomsday II defense did its job, causing many turnovers. The Rams managed 118 yards total offense, a mere 22 on the ground. Staubach called it "the most perfect football game we ever had as Cowboys."

Super Bowl X

Sunday January 18, 1976

@ Orange Bowl	**1**	**2**	**3**	**4**	**Total**
Dallas Cowboys	7	3	0	7	17
Pittsburgh Steelers	7	0	0	14	21

MVP Steeler's Lynn Swann

Super Bowl X marked a contrast of the NFL's two most popular teams – the white-and-silver–clad team from the plains of Texas versus the all-black-clad team from the coal-mining area of Pennsylvania. Dallas would be the **first wild-card team ever to make the finals** while it would also be the first matchup between the franchises. The Cowboys had never played the Pittsburgh Steelers.

The January 18, 1976, game played in Miami's Orange Bowl before 80,187 fans presented a bout between two future Hall of Fame quarterbacks – Staubach and Terry Bradshaw. It was also a duel between two of the toughest defenses in football – the Cowboys' Doomsday II and the Steelers' Iron Curtain. And it matched the wits of the two finest coaches in the game – Landry and Pittsburgh's Chuck Noll.

Though the Steelers' 21-17 win wasn't cinched until the last few plays, the experience advantage lay with the Steelers. They were a unit of veterans – most of them playing at least five years together – while the Cowboys had blended 12 young players into their lineup.

The Steelers were the best defense the Cowboys faced all season. They hounded Staubach into seven sacks and forced him into three interceptions. They also blocked a field goal attempt that led to a safety. The physical play of cornerback Mel Blount took playmaker receiver Golden Richards out of the game.

Bradshaw's play was brilliant. He finished the game with 9 out of 19 pass completions for 209 yards and two touchdowns with no interceptions. He added another 16 yards rushing.

Lynn Swann, who had suffered from a concussion two weeks prior in their AFC championship game with Oakland, wasn't sure he was going to play until he was challenged by Cowboy safety Cliff Harris during bowl week. "I'm not going to hurt anyone intentionally," said Harris. "But getting hit again while he's running a pass route must be in the back of Swann's mind."

Swann responded, "I read what Harris said. He was trying to intimidate me. He said I'd be afraid out there. He needn't worry. He doesn't know Lynn Swann. He can't scare me or the team. I said to myself, 'The hell with it. I'm going to play.'" Swann caught four passes for 161 yards and became the first receiver to win the game's MVP award.

"Maybe the best Super Bowl ever played," sportscaster Jack Whitaker claimed afterward. Whitaker also called Bradshaw's 64-yard touchdown pass to Swann with 4:50 remaining "the greatest pass in Super Bowl history." On the play, Harris was on a safety blitz, leaving cornerback Mark Washington to cover Swann alone. Bradshaw suffered a concussion as he was hit while throwing the ball on the play, forcing him out of the game.

"We expected to win Super Bowl X," said Renfro. "Until the end, we felt we were a team of destiny."

Game-film evidence demonstrated the strong defensive play of Renfro, who held big Pittsburgh receiver John Stallworth to two receptions for eight yards. Mel came up many times to make tackles or receive blocks from Franco Harris and Rocky Bleier while supporting run defense for Doomsday II.

The Cowboys had their opportunities to win, but their conservative offensive game plan played into the physical play of the

Steelers. "They were the best team we ever played," said Staubach. "Their defensive team, I think, was the best defense that's ever played in the NFL."

Even so, with 12 seconds to go in the game, Staubach's perfect pass to Percy Howard in the end zone would have won the Super Bowl for the Cowboys, if the officials had made the interference call. The Steelers were not called for one penalty the entire game. The game ended with another Hail Mary pass to Drew Pearson, which was intercepted in the end zone by Glen Edwards.

Despite the loss, Coach Landry was encouraged with the 1975 Cowboys, the team with the "dirty dozen" newcomers. He felt it was the best group he ever had from the standpoint of character, morale, spirit and teamwork. He looked forward to their future.

23

1976 and 1977

1976	11-4-0		
S12	Eagles	W	27-7
S19	@Saints	W	24-6
S26	Colts	W	30-27
O3	@Seahawks	W	28-13
O10	@Giants	W	24-14
O17	@Cardinals	L	17-21
O24	Bears	W	31-21
O31	@Redskins	W	20-7
N7	Giants	W	9-3
N15	Bills	W	17-10
N21	@Falcons	L	10-17
N25	Cardinals	W	19-14
D5	@Eagles	W	26-7
D12	Redskins	L	14-27
	Playoffs		
D19	Rams	L	12-14

The Staubach-Longley Conflict

In 1976, the Cowboys had signed Arizona State's Danny White. White was the kind of disciplined athlete Landry liked. At the end of training camp, Clint Longley – vying for the starting quarterback position – found himself as a third-stringer. He was resentful and built a wall between himself, starter Roger Staubach and their coach.

Staubach got into a scuffle with Longley at the Cowboys' training camp away from the practice field, after Longley had mouthed off at Drew Pearson and Staubach. Pearson said Staubach put "one of those Vietnam holds on Longley – that Kung Fu fighting." Soon enough, Longley was down on the ground with his feet in the air. The fight was over.

The next day, Longley sought revenge. He was waiting for Staubach in the locker room. When Staubach was rushing to get to the field and was pulling his shoulder pads over his head, Longley decked him with a "sucker" punch.

Staubach was caught off guard and fell back on a set of weight scales, hitting his head – with blood gushing everywhere. They wrestled on the concrete floor before big Randy White separated them. Once White let them go, Longley, with blood all over himself, took off, passing Landry on the way out without saying anything. Longley had already packed his car to leave.

The trainer placed a bandage on Staubach's head against his objection: "I'm OK! I'm all right! Everything's fine!" Staubach took off running toward the dorm to get Longley before his teammates interceded and stopped him. Landry didn't tolerate the incident. That was the end of Longley as a Cowboy. He was traded to San Diego.

Injuries

The Cowboys started out the year winning games on big plays. Staubach was having his best season as the team depended on his passing game before he broke his finger against the Bears in the seventh game. Staubach took a hit from defensive back Virgil Livers' helmet when he scored on a four-yard touchdown run. Danny White came in and threw two touchdowns to win 31-21. The Cowboy record was 6-1, but their passing game began to falter. By the end of the season, the whole offense struggled when both fullback Robert Newhouse and receiver Preston Pearson ailed with injuries. The Cowboys had a good 11-3 record, but literally limped into the playoffs.

In the playoff game, the Cowboys were leading 10-7 into the fourth quarter, but gave up a last-minute touchdown, losing 14-12.

The injured Dallas needed a running game. "Just one running back, and we'd be the best damn team God ever gave breath to," defensive end Harvey Martin moaned.

Age and the wear and tear on a knee caught up with Mel Renfro in 1976. "I remember in practice before the Buffalo game in a one-and-one coverage drill, my right knee popped," said Renfro, who would turn 35 on December 30. "I missed the last six games of the season. My knee would swell up and it continually needed to be drained."

"Dr. Marvin Knight, the Cowboys' team doctor, refused to operate. He advised me: 'Mel, you need to retire.' I told him, 'No – I need to have my knee fixed first.'"

The Super Bowl Season

1977	(15-2-0)		
S18	@Vikings	W	16-10
S25	Giants	W	41-21
O2	Buccaneers	W	23-7
O9	@Cardinals	W	30-24
O16	Redskins	W	34-16
O23	@Eagles	W	16-10
O30	Lions	W	37-0

1977	**(15-2-0)**		
N6	@Giants	W	24-10
N14	Cardinals	L	17-24
N20	@Steelers	L	13-28
N27	@Redskins	W	14-7
D4	Eagles	W	24-14
D12	@49ers	W	42-35
D18	Broncos	W	14-6
	Playoffs		
D26	Bears	W	37-7
J1	Vikings	W	23-6
	Super Bowl XII		
J15	Broncos	W	27-10

Mel's Knee Surgery

Mel Renfro had missed the last six games of the 1976 season and refused to retire from professional football until he had his troubled right knee repaired.

Chuck Dekeado, Renfro's agent, contacted the Oakland Raiders' team doctor for knee surgery. Renfro flew to Los Angeles in March 1977 and had arthroscopic surgery done by Dr. Robert Rosenfeld at Cedars-Sinai Hospital. "I had an epidural anesthetic and could hear the doctors talking during surgery," Renfro said. "They said, 'Look at all the snow in there. This surgery should have been done four or five years ago.'"

After the surgery, Renfro bought a house near his family when he returned to Portland to rehabilitate his right knee. "Within a few months, I was running five miles every day," he said.

Renfro felt good entering training camp, but the early understanding was Coach Landry was going to hold him out of preseason play to further his healing. Nevertheless, for whatever reason, Coach Tom Landry played him three quarters of the preseason opener game and all of the next three. "I continued to grade out 95, 96 out of a possible 100 points," Mel said.

In the preseason finale at Seattle, however, Renfro sat the entire game. He was upset. "My mom, dad and brothers all traveled to Seattle to see me play," Renfro said. "It was a huge personal disappointment."

The week before the 1977 regular-season opener at Minnesota, defensive backs coach Gene Stallings spoke to Renfro. "He told me, 'We aren't going to start you,'" said Mel. "Coach Tom Landry decided to go with Aaron Kyle, who was much younger and healthier. Although I was pissed, I felt I could still play. I knew my knee wasn't 100 percent, but I didn't think it would last the whole season. But it was Coach Landry's decision."

"With Mel's knees and age, it's going to be pretty hard for him to play consistently anymore," Landry told the Dallas media.

"At that point, I knew it was my last year," concluded Mel. "But after that, what bothered me most was, when they would send me in, it was always late in the game, when I was cold and at a crucial time in tough third-down situations."

Renfro recalled a midseason game against St. Louis. "It was cold and late in a close game," he said. "They put me in at corner to cover All-Pro receiver Mel Gray. I could see quarterback Jim Hart licking his chops, so I mentioned to safety Charley Waters that I was going to need some help in coverage. At about 40 yards, Gray ran by me to catch the winning touchdown pass. There was no help over the top. Waters had drifted over to help out Cliff Harris. I chased Gray through the end zone, then circled the field back to the bench. I didn't play or practice another down until Super Bowl XII."

Tony Dorsett

In 1977, free agency was in effect for the NFL and the likelihood of higher salaries came into play with the new collective-bargaining agreement. The Cowboys' woefully inadequate running game that ended the 1976 season prematurely needed to be addressed, and General Manager Tex Schramm and vice president/player personnel Gil Brandt proved themselves again.

The Cowboys traded four draft picks to the Seattle Seahawks for the second choice in the 1977 draft. It was contingent on Tampa Bay selecting USC's running back Ricky Bell with the first pick. That would leave the Cowboys with the selection of Heisman Trophy winner Tony Dorsett, the running back out of Pittsburgh.

Anthony "Tony" Dorsett was a three-time first-team All-American (1973, 1975, 1976) for Coach Johnny Majors' University of Pittsburgh Panthers football team. In 1973, Dorsett became the first freshman in 29 years to be selected first-team All-American (Army's Doc Blanchard was the previous one in 1944). Dorsett was second in the nation in rushing with 1,586 yards in 11 games and led his team to its first winning season in 10 years. Against Notre Dame his junior year, Dorsett had 303 yards to break his Panther single-game rushing record. As a senior, he had a total of 290 yards against Notre Dame. He ran 61 yards on the first play of the season and added 129 more by the end of Pitt's 31-10 win against the Irish. As a senior in 1976, he led the Panthers to a national title. He won the Heisman, the Maxwell, the Walter Camp and Associated Press awards for Player of the Year. He finished his college career with 6,082 total rushing yards, then an NCAA record. Dorsett is considered one of the best running backs in college history. He became the first player to win the college championship one year, then win the Super Bowl the next.

Many NFL owners were stunned with the trade in which four draft picks were exchanged for a future Hall of Famer to a team that had the best winning record in the last decade. But Seattle General

Manager John Thompson seemed happy because he didn't have to pay the top draft choice $1 million. Dorsett's agent, Mike Trope, managed a $1.1-million deal for his player.

In Pittsburgh, Dorsett was more famous than the mayor. He found it hard to adjust to the starkly different social scene that existed in Dallas. His extravagant flair for cars (a midnight black Porsche), clothes (full-length mink coat) and the night life in the North Dallas bars, not to mention his affinity for wearing dark glasses in the evening, turned heads. After an assault charge for slugging a bartender, which was immediately dropped, Dorsett was forced to tone down his act, although he was unhappy with his restrictions.

Renfro's observation on Dorsett was noted by Peter Golenbock in *Landry's Boys:* "Tony came out of the East Coast, from Pittsburgh, where he lived by a different set of rules. In Pittsburgh, everybody loved him. In Dallas and the South, although blacks were treated OK, he couldn't do what he did back home, and so Tony had bitterness. Even though he was popular in the sense that people liked his football performance, he still couldn't live the way he was used to living."

After a slow start due to injuries and getting used to the demanding Landry practices, Dorsett found the field. He was special. The Cowboys were 12-2 in the regular season, scoring 340 points. Dorsett was the game-breaking piece the Cowboys needed in their offense. The running game they desired was back. Dorsett could run inside and outside. The NFL's Offensive Rookie of the Year gained 1,007 yards with 12 TDs on 208 carries.

Staubach was back to his old form and had a great year. He completed 210 of 361 passes for 2,620 yards during the regular season. With the offense balanced, it took the pressure off him, along with the aid of the tough and stingy Doomsday II defense.

The Cowboys won their first eight games and dominated the NFC. Quarterback Staubach; ends Billy Joe DuPree and Drew Pearson; defensive backs Cliff Harris and Charlie Waters; tackles

Harvey Martin and Randy White; and kicker Efren Herrera had Pro Bowl seasons.

In the opening playoff game with the Bears, the Cowboys rolled to a 37-7 win, and they beat the Vikings 23-6 at Texas Stadium to earn their fourth Super Bowl.

Super Bowl XII Champions

Sunday, January 15, 1978

@Super Dome	1	2	3	4	Total
Dallas Cowboys	10	3	7	7	27
Denver Broncos	0	0	10	0	10

Co-MVPs Randy White & Harvey Martin

Super Bowl XII was the first time the game was played in a domed stadium, the Louisiana Superdome in New Orleans. The game featured the Cowboys' current quarterback, Staubach, against their former quarterback, Craig Morton.

The Cowboys' defense dominated most of the game, forcing eight turnovers and allowing only eight pass completions by the Broncos for 61 yards. Two of the interceptions led to 10 first- quarter points. Dallas expanded its lead to 20-3 in the third quarter after Bruce Johnson made a diving catch in the end zone for a 45-yard TD.

Denver cut the deficit to 20-10 after an ineffective Morton was replaced in the third quarter, but the Cowboys put the game out of reach when Robert Newhouse threw a halfback pass for a 29-yard touchdown to Golden Richards.

Renfro's Last Game – a Super Bowl Win

During the 1977 season, Mel was a reserve. His knee injury prevented him from playing the final six games of the season. He was in the Super Bowl for the fourth time, yet now he was hobbling along the sidelines.

Starting cornerback Benny Barnes went down with an injury and reserve corner Mark Washington, a former starter, was dinged up and not ready to play. The coaches tabbed Mel for one last burst of action.

"Coach Stallings looked up and down the sidelines," recounted Mel. "He said, 'Hey, Fro, can you go?' I played three quarters and tried to resemble a football player out there."

With the Super Bowl co-MVPs Harvey Martin and Randy White harassing Craig Morton, "that helped a good deal," Renfro said. "It was a great way for me to go out. Not many players go out with a Super Bowl victory. But I knew the knee was bad, and I couldn't play anymore."

NFL Statistics for Mel Renfro 1964–77

Kickoff Returns

Year	Ret	Yds	Avg	Long	TD
1964	40	1017	25.4	64	0
1965	21	630	30	100	1
1966	19	487	25.6	87	1
1967	5	112	22.4	30	0
Total	85	2246	26.4	100	2

Mel Renfro's Cowboy Career Record: 26.4 yard kickoff return average

Punt Returns

Year	Ret	Yds	Avg	Long	TD
1964	32	418	13.1	69	1
1965	24	145	6.0	35	0
1966	21	123	5.9	38	0
1967	3	-1	-0.3	7	0

Year	Ret	Yds	Avg	Long	TD
1969	15	80	5.3	34	0
1970	13	77	5.9	29	0
Total	109	842	7.7	69	1

Defensive

Year	Fum	Td	Int	Yds	Avg	Td
1964	4	1	7	110	15.7	1
1965	3	1	2	92	46	1
1966	2	1	2	57	28.5	0
1967	0	0	7	38	5.4	0
1968	0	0	3	5	1.7	0
1969	2	0	10	118	11.8	0
1970	1	0	4	3	0.8	0
1971	0	0	4	11	2.8	0
1972	0	0	1	0	0.0	0
1973	0	0	2	65	32.5	1
1974	0	0	1	6	6	0
1975	0	0	4	70	17.5	0
1976	0	0	3	23	7.7	0
1977	0	0	2	28	14	0
Total	12	3	52	626	12	3

Mel Renfro's Cowboys Career Records

- 52 interceptions
- 626 interception return yards

Honor Roll

- 4-Time All-Pro

- 10-Time Pro Bowl
- 3-Time All-NFC
- 2 Super Bowl titles
- 4 NFC Championships
- 9 Division Titles
- Pro Football Hall of Fame

24

Retirement

MEL RENFRO WAS 36 AS THE 1978 NFL SEASON APPROACHED. HE knew his time as an NFL player was either nearing an end or over.

"In the spring of 1978, after the Cowboys let me know they weren't going to re-sign me, Coach Jack Pardee of the Redskins contacted me and flew me to Washington," Renfro said. "He told me, 'Mel, if you can play, we will sign you. Otherwise, we will hire you as a coach.'"

Mel was flattered and gave the offer some thought. Even the backup plan – that the Redskins would hire him as a coach – gave him a sense of security for his future. But before Mel could sort out his options, a reporter from Dallas got wind of the offer and called him. It forced Mel to respond: "Yeah, I talked to them. I haven't made a decision yet."

Feeling rushed into making a decision and concerned that his damaged leg wouldn't hold up another season, Mel announced his retirement as a player the next day.

"In the back of my mind, I felt a loyalty through my 14 years with the Cowboys," he said. "And going to the Redskins, our biggest division rival, didn't make sense to me at the time. I thought, 'This is going to create a mess in the media. To hell with it.'"

Renfro had played 22 years of football – four years in high school, four years in college and 14 years in the NFL. It should have been the time for him to capitalize on the reputation he created for himself. It should have been the best time of his life, but it wasn't. Mel had waited until retirement before he gave serious thought to life after football.

Even so, Mel thought he was ready for his retirement financially. He had some money saved and had invested in a partnership in some popular fried chicken restaurants, feeling the future was bright and prosperous.

"I hung around hoping (Dallas head coach Tom) Landry would hire me as a coach," Mel recalled. "I was disappointed it didn't materialize."

Renfro knew former players Dan Reeves, Mike Ditka, Jerry Tubbs and Dick Nolan were all hired by Landry as assistant coaches. After 14 years playing for the Cowboys and being a big part of the Doomsday Defense, Mel felt he had solid credentials for a coaching job.

It was wishful thinking. Mel didn't discuss his future after football with Landry or ask for an opportunity to coach on his staff. He avoided the issue. "I had never approached Landry with the idea of hiring me as an assistant coach," Renfro said. And he didn't after announcing his retirement, either.

Up to that time, the Cowboys didn't have any black coaches on their staff. Hiring black coaches was one of the many issues that were slow to evolve in the South.

Healing from Football

"I didn't miss football," Mel said. "It took me about six months to heal and get it out of my system. The aches and pains I'd lived with year after year stopped. My ankles, knees, elbows and neck didn't hurt anymore. At that time, I knew I didn't miss it. But what I did miss were the friendships with the players. We were a pretty tight group. You miss those things."

Scouting

Though a coaching job wasn't in the works, Dallas vice president/ player personnel Gil Brandt hired Renfro as a scout.

"I was scouting and evaluating college players for $1,000 a month – $700 take-home pay," he said. "It was a pay cut of almost 86 percent from my time as a player. I was on the road all the time, evaluating and writing up and filing scouting reports. I would leave on Monday, return on Saturday, then be gone again on Monday."

The scouting job lasted eight months, until training camp started in July 1978.

"I was left behind with just the secretary," Renfro said. "I became the 'gofer,' sending boxes and trunks to Thousand Oaks. At that time, I realized the job had no financial future for me. I couldn't see myself doing that for another few years. I told myself, 'No!' And I just walked out."

Henderson's Honey Fried Chicken

Shortly after the 1976 divorce from his wife Pat, Renfro began a relationship with 19-year-old Mechelle Simmons.

"When we were dating, I got to meet her folks," he said. "Mechelle was the step-daughter of Herman Henderson, who owned three popular and successful fried chicken stores in Dallas. Mr. Henderson was looking to retire, and I may have been recommended by him to be included in a four-person partnership to buy him out, with the idea of opening more stores."

Renfro agreed to be part of the ownership group.

"We each contributed $15,000 and immediately changed the

name to Henderson's Honey Fried Chicken," he said. "I was in charge of one store, which was almost a "cash cow." Our store was doing extremely well with our sizable deposits into the bank, when we had a major dispute.

"One of the partners came by to audit how things were going. He couldn't believe how well our store was doing. He felt I should move the money into his bank account and take back some equipment that I had ordered. It upset me so much, I complained. We dissolved the partnership and I was left with a single store to run."

The business began to struggle.

"Within six months, I knew I was in trouble," Renfro said. "I made a couple of bad decisions. I held it too long and I hired some bad people. I had to close the store and was forced into personal bankruptcy. I lost all of my investment. It was a dark time for me."

Religion

By 1979, Mel turned to religion.

"Although I grew up in the church, I hadn't attended in a long time until Mechelle and I went together to her church, the Believers Tabernacle," said Mel. "With all the negative things going on in my life, I decided I needed a change. I've always prayed, but now I wanted to be saved and born again."

Through his church attendance, Renfro felt a revival of spirit.

"At first I had a warm and fuzzy feeling," he said. "Then I felt that I had been cleansed. I felt a contentment for the first time in a long while. I searched my soul and through my struggles I had my first vision for a Bridge Foundation for disadvantaged kids. Growing up, I felt the parks were my safe havens and the ball fields were there for kids to express ourselves."

When the couple was married in 1979, Mechelle was 21, attractive and a nice dresser. It didn't take long before Mel realized their difference in age and values would become a stumbling block in their relationship.

"She wasn't ready to be married because her vows didn't mean much to her," Renfro said. "She still wanted to chase around."

A son, Jason, was born October 16, 1981. Mel and Mechelle separated that year and by 1983 were divorced.

Miller's Magnum Beer

In 1980, Renfro was offered a job by Miller Beer Company as a brand manager to promote and sell its malt liquor called "Magnum." Cowboy teammate Willie Townes was already a manager in the company's sales program.

"It didn't help matters that I was working for a beer company," said Mel. "Even though for years I had been a notorious beer drinker, I had stopped drinking before I was offered the job."

Feeling conflicted, Mel sought counsel from his pastor. "Realizing I was 'down and out' financially and desperate for work," said Mel, "the pastor's limited advice was: 'Mel, pray about it first and then go with your gut instincts.'"

Mel took the job with a salary much higher than what he was making as a scout for the Cowboys. "They also gave me a company car and expense account," he said. "I was on the management team, dealing with sales and distribution. Magnum's main consumers were black people between the ages of 19 and 49. I was in charge of the programs that would stimulate its sales."

The position did not work out well for Mel. The job forced him to be social, take clients out, and of course, Mel felt he had to drink the beer to promote his product. "I would come home with a hangover and would need time to dry out," said Mel. "I physically couldn't handle it. I lasted only a year and a half with Miller's."

25

Ring of Honor – Ticket Scandal

IN THE FALL OF 1981, MEL RENFRO GOT THE CALL FROM DALLAS PRESident/general manager Tex Schramm. He would be the fifth retired player to be inducted in the Cowboy Ring of Honor.

The Dallas Cowboy Ring of Honor, a ring around Texas Stadium in Irving, Texas, and currently around Cowboys Stadium in Arlington, Texas, honors former players, coaches and club officials who made outstanding contributions to the Dallas Cowboys football organization. The Ring of Honor began in 1975 on a day designated in Dallas as Bob Lilly Day. The team unveiled Lilly's name and jersey number beneath the press box during halftime. As the first honoree, Lilly, who retired in July 1975 after 14 years, donned his Cowboy uniform once more and graciously accepted the honor, along with numerous other gifts, which included a car, a gun and a hunting dog. As the first inductee, Lilly has the added distinction of returning to present each new member in the Ring of Honor. Only nine players received the honor during the first three decades of the Cowboys' existence, making it a coveted accolade, true to the dream envisioned by Schramm, its creator.

"I was sitting in my office at Miller Beer," said Mel, "when out of the blue, I got a call from Tex."

"Mel," Schramm said, "we are going to induct you in the Ring of Honor."

"I was surprised," said Mel, remembering his bad feelings from the many times he and Schramm butted heads. "Wow! I didn't think it would happen. I was on Cloud Nine. It felt like the problems of the past were washed away."

Lilly called later to congratulate him. "You are going into the Ring of Honor, and later you are going into the Pro Hall of Fame," Lilly told his former teammate.

"That also made me feel better," said Mel.

Halftime October 25, 1981

Renfro joined the Ring of Honor during a home game against the Miami Dolphins. "It had been three years since I had been on the field," said Mel. "It felt great. I had a flashback of the past and a surge of adrenaline coming down the ramp of Cowboys Stadium."

After his introduction by Lilly, Renfro accepted the silver-pewter Ring of Honor bowl as the team unveiled "RENFRO" and his jersey No. 20 beneath the press box. It felt special for the fifth inductee. Renfro expressed his thanks: "To the Cowboy organization, my teammates and the fans who were supportive of me."

It was a big honor for Mel. He felt great about it until a few months later, when he felt the world crashing down on him – again.

The Ticket Scandal

In December 1981, there was a report on national television of a "Los Angeles–Dallas Super Bowl ticket scandal. The report said Renfro "was the 'king-pin' in Dallas, with a network of ticket scalpers." The two alleged ticket-scalping events occurred during the Super Bowl XII season in 1977 and the following season when Mel was employed as a Cowboy scout.

The report got Mel's attention. "It was untrue there was a network," he explained. "I called the TV station immediately to refute the network charge. It came from the same people at the Dallas station that always had access to me during my playing days. They knew I lived in the area, but they never returned my call.

"Three weeks later, a New York TV crew showed up at my doorstep asking about the ticket scalping. I was caught off-guard, but I wanted to voice my side. I didn't want to take the entire blame."

Renfro told that reporter that in 1977 and '78, "four of us players and an assistant coach were selling the tickets that were offered to us. The NFL was desperate in its desire to sell tickets to the Super Bowls, so players and coaches were offered as many as 20 tickets each at discounted prices. We paid $25–30 apiece for them and in turn were paid $150-200 each by a ticket vendor out of LA."

Much to Mel's dismay, the TV interview was played the day before the Super Bowl and focused primarily on the "Cowboy players and a coach involved" quote, which caught the eyes and ears of Schramm. It would be an understatement to say Mel's referencing a Cowboy coach being involved didn't sit well with the team's president and general manager.

"Things hit the fan," said Mel. "Schramm called me in, and we had a face-to-face. He told me: **'Mel, I'll die and go to hell before I see you in the Pro Football Hall of Fame.'**"

In a 2012 interview, former vice president/player personnel Gil Brandt said he was unaware of Mel's charges that Schramm delivered that threat to the former Cowboy All-Star. In defense of the general manager, Brandt said, "I knew Tex so well, and I can't believe that he would make that statement."

But in Mel's support, Brandt elaborated, "I am the biggest fan of Mel Renfro as a player and as a person. Mel worked for me as a scout. He is among the nearest and dearest people to my heart. I never worked so hard trying to get him into the Pro Football Hall of Fame. When players were selected, I used to ask (Hall of Fame director) Pete Elliott and the Dallas sportswriters, 'Who would you rather have, Mel Renfro, or whoever was going in?' My estimation was: **Mel Renfro was the most athletic player we ever had.**"

Just two months after Renfro's career was honored by the Ring of Honor celebration, he felt devastated. His Cowboy image was damaged. The threat of being blocked from the Pro Football Hall of Fame bothered him deeply and would haunt him for the next fifteen years.

Child Support Problems

Financial problems continued to plague Mel. He was taken to court in Dallas in 1982 for failure to pay $8,582 in child support. The judge was hard on him: "Do you rent?"..."Yes." "Do you own a car?"..."Yes" "That's six months in jail for you." After he spent two days in jail, Mel's boss at Miller Beer bailed him out.

In 1983, when Mel was going through hard times, he felt a depth of depression the former star athlete had never experienced. He had unpaid bills. He assumed a victim's role. "My life was pure hell," said Mel. "There were no opportunities for me. I couldn't get a job and I couldn't even get a loan to start a business."

The State of Oregon Sports Hall of Fame weekend in July 1983 became an embarrassment for Mel. Instead of enjoying the honor of being recognized as one of Oregon's top athletes, the non-payment of child support raised its legal head again. His ex-wife Pat was a police department secretary.

"I was arrested carrying my two-year old Jason off the airplane by two detectives," pointed out Mel. "An attorney friend of mine got me out of jail immediately."

"Then when I was walking into the banquet at the Red Lion with my family, two Portland policemen arrested me again," said Mel shaking his head. "'I have already been arrested,' I told them. They apologized and let me go again, if I would appear in court the next day. It was so embarrassing to me and three of my kids and a sister-in-law."

Mel went to court the next day. "Give him his $300 back," said the judge. "And let this guy go."

Not long after, Mel received a $20,000 NFL retirement package. He was able to pay back the bail money and make a final child support settlement with Pat.

Pro Hall of Fame Issues

When Tex Schramm flew the Naval Academy band to Dallas in October 1983 for Roger Staubach's Ring of Honor celebration, Mel felt it was a "slap in the face for those of us who were suffering from hardships." Mel's venting was not against his treasured friend and former teammate Staubach, but aimed toward Schramm.

The Ring of Honor event for Staubach also coincided with a spontaneous explanatory meeting when Pete Elliott spotted Mel sitting in the cabaret at the Cowboys' pre-party at the Galleria. Coincidentally, Elliott, the ex-college football coach, got his first start in 1949 on Kip Taylor's Oregon State staff, the year Tom DeSylvia, Mel's high school coach was the team captain.

The sit-down face-to-face with the Pro Hall of Fame's executive director went painfully. "Mel, you **are not** going to be inducted into the Hall of Fame," he said. "And you **know** the reason why."

There was negative gossip going around Dallas that Mel didn't hear, but his depressed state of mind didn't go without notice. "Dickie Daniels called first, offering help," remembered Mel. "'You'll be hearing from Bob Lilly,' he said, 'we got some money together, you need to get some fresh air.'"

Then Lilly called: "Mel, we are going to send you a check. You need to get a fresh start...you need to leave Dallas." Mel went to Portland.

26

Coaching

USFL LA Express

In 1983, Mel Renfro moved back to Portland. Six months later, he got a call from his friend, Dickie Daniels, who was in a management position for the second-year U.S. Football League Los Angeles Express. Daniels offered Renfro a coaching position.

Without giving it much thought, Mel jumped at the opportunity to get back into football again. He accepted the offer to coach the secondary and moved to Los Angeles before he realized John Hadl, the new head coach who replaced former Canadian Football League coach Hugh Campbell, wasn't allowed to hire his choice for that defensive coaching position.

"When I was first with the Cowboys," said Daniels in a 2013 interview, "Mel helped me with my fundamentals. He gave me a foundation. He was an excellent coach, a great teacher. Mel understood people, and he is truthful. Our players were all attracted to him."

"John Hadl resented Daniels hiring me," said Renfro. "He wanted his own guys."

It became an unresolved conflict. Mel drove to Los Angeles,

stayed in a hotel and arrived to coach for a team that played during a season that began in the spring and went through the summer.

Custody

During this time the divorce from Mechelle was finalized, and it forced Mel to make another lifestyle adjustment – a blessing to him. He had to "man up" to a big responsibility – gaining custody of his son. "When Jason was 3 ½, he was literally dropped on my doorstep in LA by his mother," said Mel. "Mechelle wanted to get on with her life and turned Jason over to me – no custody hearing, no alimony.

"I had to find a townhouse and hire a nanny to help care for him. Five days a week, I would get up at five in the morning, have her take him to day care by seven and then bring him back by 7:30 that night."

1984 Season

Prior to the 1984 season, J. William Oldenburg bought the Express, and he and general manager Don Klosterman assembled a great crop of young talent. Tops on the list was BYU quarterback Steve Young, who signed a whopping $40-million lifetime annuity contract. Young also had the benefit of young offensive linemen in Baylor's Mark Adickes, Texas' Mike Ruether, Oregon's Gary Zimmerman, and former Oregon State and NFL veteran Jeff Hart.

Despite playing before small average crowds of 15,000 in the huge Los Angeles Coliseum, through Young's passing and leadership, the Express earned a playoff berth. They beat the defending champion Michigan Panthers in the longest game in professional football history, a three-overtime, 93 ½-minute affair in exhausting heat, 27-21. "Our guys were really tired," said Mel. "Their tongues were hanging out."

The Express proceeded to the Western Conference final, where they fell to the Arizona Wranglers 35-23. Their final record was 10-8.

Oldenburg declared bankruptcy after the 1984 season, turning the franchise over to the league. As soon as new management took over for the 1985 season, Hadl fired Renfro.

That ended Mel's first coaching experience. Meanwhile, the Express couldn't find an owner. With their huge salary burden and dreadful attendance, the Express barely survived the 1985 season. As a result of many failures and problems, the league folded in 1987, losing $163 million. Daniels returned to the NFL as the personnel director for the Redskins.

Custody Again

In the meantime, Mechelle had a change of heart. She had a warrant processed to get Jason back. The policeman delivering the document went to the wrong apartment, but it eventually found its way to Mel. He and Jason returned to Portland. Through negotiations with their attorneys, Mel agreed to turn Jason back to his mother in Dallas.

The separation lasted but two years before Jason was back in Mel's custody. "My second year with the St. Louis Cardinals, his mother turned him back over to me again," said Mel. "Jason was too much for her to handle."

A recent high school graduate from Mechelle's family with time on his hands agreed to come to St. Louis and help care for Jason while Mel was busy coaching. After Mel's coaching stint was over, Mel took the young man, Jason's babysitter, back to Dallas.

The St. Louis Cardinals

In 1986, when Gene Stallings took over as head coach of the St. Louis Cardinals, with offensive stars Neil Lomax and Roy Green, he hired Renfro as his defensive backfield coach. Stallings had coached defensive backs for the Cowboys for 14 seasons from 1972 to 1984.

The Cardinals' defensive stats improved significantly from the 1985 season, allowing only 21 passing TDs and improving on the number of passing yards given up defensively.

But the defensive improvement didn't continue. While the 1987 season found the offense improving and the Cardinals winning more games and placing second in the NFC division, the defensive stats reverted to 1985 levels. The position with the Cardinals wasn't a good fit for Mel. His playing experience and knowledge of the NFL should have been an asset, but it wasn't well respected. When he offered input of his own, it was often met with resistance. Even Stallings became critical and would interrupt some of his drills. It became very frustrating for Renfro, who became singled out as a poor "staff member."

He was fired at the end of the season. In the aftermath, Mel **was not** considered for another coaching job, pro or college. He was replaced by Dennis Thurman, the former USC All-American who was drafted by the Cowboys to replace Renfro at his retirement in 1977, and who played under Stallings for eight seasons (1978–85). The opportunity led Thurman to a 23-year coaching career with the Cardinals, USC, the Baltimore Ravens and the New York Jets. In 2015, at age 58, Thurman was named the defensive coordinator for the Buffalo Bills.

LA and Portland

In 1988, Mel and Jason, now seven, moved to LA after his release by the Cardinals. Mel seized the opportunity to renew his relationship with his older sons, Melvin Jr., now 24, and Tony, 23. They lived in an apartment together in Hollywood for two months. Meanwhile, daughter Cynthia, 20, was in college at USC.

Mel moved back to Portland and sold cars in 1989 and '90.

"I worked for six months with Ron Tonkin Ford as a salesman," he said. "It was a high-pressure operation – too much for me. Later, I worked with Artie Wilson, an older former Negro Leagues and Pacific Coast League baseball player, selling cars in Gladstone, a southern suburb of Portland. I liked it better there. It was more relaxing for me."

Las Vegas

In 1991, Renfro received a call from Chuck Dekeado. A sports bar owner in Las Vegas wanted a "name" attraction to enhance his operation. Together Mel and Dekeado could manage the bar, with a buy-out opportunity in the future. They took advantage of the offer hoping it would work out for both of them. The bar, located in the west-side neighborhood of Las Vegas at 901 West Owens, would be called Mel Renfro's Out of Bounds Sports Lounge.

The business featured a dozen slot machines, two bartenders, a couple of waitresses and a cook to provide food for breakfast, lunch and dinner.

"But things didn't work out for Dekeado," said Mel. "He got fired the first three or four months, leaving the management to me. I began working 12–14 hours per day, six days a week. Jason and I lived in an apartment for two weeks before I rented a house."

Something else changed in Mel's life.

"I met Evett, an attractive clerk at Costco, buying groceries," he said. "Then she started showing up at the bar. We hit it off and were married within the year in Las Vegas."

Evett had three young children of her own, Scott, Malia and Demarrie. With Jason, who was now school age, there were four young children in the home.

On May 1, 1992, when Central Los Angeles was smoldering from the aftermath of the Rodney King trial which acquitted four LA police officers, disturbances flared up in other cities. Most of the demonstrations were peaceful, except for Atlanta, San Francisco and Las Vegas. The riots caused an estimated $2 million in damages and resulted in 50 deaths and thousands of injuries. A small scale outbreak in Las Vegas caused the arson of Mel Renfro's Out of Bounds Lounge. Las Vegas had gang activity when the Crips and the Bloods spilled over to Las Vegas from LA. Two dozen businesses were destroyed and looted. The Out of Bounds Sports Lounge was gutted by fire on May 10, when a well-armed crowd set the blaze and then used gunfire to keep police and fire crews from responding to the alarm.

With the lounge destroyed, Mel resigned and the owner gave up the property a few months later.

The Bridge

In 1993, Mel rented a U-Haul, returned to Portland and went back to church.

"Something was missing," said Mel. "I prayed a lot, and I sensed God told me to give back to the community."

Mel often remembered his kid brother Raye, a great high school athlete, who was a sad casualty in his day. His encounter with the law in the spring of his senior year derailed his aspirations to play big-time college football. "Raye got lost in the shuffle, fell through the cracks and passed away at a young age," said Mel. "Instead of people helping him, they turned their backs on him."

With that inspiration, Mel got involved with Pastor Donald Frazier's Mt. Sinai Baptist Church, who partnered with him in a ministry called The Bridge. The original mission statement was to mix religion, mentoring, counseling, athletics and arts in addition to offering help with substance abuse.

"A group of men from the church would visit the Portland's

Youth Detention Center to counsel young men," said Renfro. "For two years, we did the follow-up visits with them, **to do the right thing.**" During its short duration, Mel's strengths mentoring with athletics weren't realized as the needed facilities had not yet been developed.

Mel Renfro's Legends Honey-Fried Chicken

In 1994, with aid from an early $25,000 NFL pension settlement in 1992, Mel opened **The Legends**, a small chicken restaurant on the corner of NE Williams and Cook in his childhood neighborhood. "I tried to reproduce the Henderson's Honey-Fried Chicken formula," said Mel. "Although people were lined up outside the door when we opened, we were not able to reproduce the proper taste. It had something to do with how the lard was added. Business suffered and within a year, I had to shut it down."

27

Induction into the Pro Football Hall of Fame

In 1996, Mel Renfro was inducted into the Pro Football Hall of Fame. Jean-Jacques Taylor of the *Dallas Morning News* captured the setting for Mel on his special day: "On a crisp January morning early in 1996, Mel opened the door to his Portland home on Northeast Mallory and stared at the wonderment of the thick blanket of snow covering his neighborhood. 'It was so beautiful and the snow was so fresh that it seemed to be an omen,' Renfro said. 'It was a winter wonderland, and it was a magnificent setting for something good to happen.'"

A Chicago radio station called. He had been accepted. On July 27 in Canton, Ohio, Renfro would become the seventh Cowboy and the 186th player inducted. The 1996 class would also include Chargers wide receiver Charlie Joiner, Redskin Coach Joe Gibbs, Cardinals tackle Dan Dierdorf and Lions guard Lou Creekmur.

Four times in 14 years, Renfro had been a finalist for induction into the Hall of Fame. Each time, he had failed to get enough votes from the selection committee.

"It was bittersweet for me," said Mel. "It was difficult for me the first two times I was nominated, because I had the credentials. It really hurt me and my family.

"At first, I just assumed I was going into the Hall of Fame, especially after Bob Lilly and Roger Staubach got in. But the hurtful threat by Tex Schramm following the ticket scandal and Pete Elliott's sit-me-down talk that 'I would **never** get into the Hall' haunted me with doubt for 15 long years. It also crossed my mind to deny the offer (of induction) when it came as a personal statement. But I remembered what Lilly told me: 'Mel, when it comes, don't be bitter; accept it with joy.'

"As things settled in, I **did** accept the induction with joy, and received it with appreciation. Life after football had been an arduous journey, but the confirmation of being selected to the Pro Football Hall of Fame became an adrenaline flow that never ended. I looked forward to it. I was still on 'cloud nine' when I asked former coach Tom Landry to introduce me."

People kept calling Mel to congratulate him.

"It was just the way Sam Huff, a Hall of Fame linebacker, told me it would be," said Mel. "That I would be thrilled by all the attention following the announcement, and that I would be in awe at the induction weekend at the Hall of Fame Game in July. I told Sam, 'I can't wait.'"

Mel credits the tenacity of *Dallas Morning News* columnist Frank Luksa in lobbying for his getting on the final ballot and gaining induction in 1996. The Hall of Fame committee is made of representatives from each NFL city. Those reps make cases for players from their areas. Every year for 15 years, Luksa made the Renfro case during the committee's Super Bowl meeting. Finally, on Luksa's last year on the committee and Renfro's last on the regular ballot, Renfro got in. "No one raised an objection about Renfro's worth," said Luksa. "A bad sign now I think on it, because it meant anti-Cowboy minds were fixed." For a nine-year stretch, from Roger Staubach's induction in 1985 until Randy White's induction in 1994, there were no Cowboy players inducted.

Perhaps it wasn't coincidental that Tex Schramm – with whom Renfro had several run-ins – was fired as the Cowboy general manager in 1989, and that Pro Hall of Fame executive director Pete Elliott retired in 1995, the year before Renfro was selected.

"It took me a long time to get inducted," Mel said. "Without getting into specifics, the Cowboys never promoted me," Mel said. "There were some things they did to keep me out of things. I no longer have any regrets about things that happened during my playing days. My born-again Christian status has washed away the bitterness. Right now, God is in control of this. Before I came to the Lord, I was disappointed, frustrated and wondering what was going on. I think God has a plan for where I go."

After he was notified of his induction, Renfro made plans for the whole family to go to Canton.

"Evett and I had been struggling with our marriage and had decided to separate, but we agreed to go our own ways after the ceremony in August," said Mel. "Evett returned to Houston, while my sights were set on Dallas." They divorced in 1997.

The Hall of Fame

The Hall opened in Canton, Ohio, on September 7, 1963, with 17 charter inductees. Canton was selected as its location because the NFL had been founded there in 1920. During the league's first few years the Canton Bulldogs were a successful NFL team. Canton lobbied the NFL in 1962 to have the Hall built in their city. The museum building, which has undergone three major expansions, now covers 82,307 square feet and has a yearly average attendance of 200,000.

By their 50th anniversary in 2013, the Hall had inducted a total of

280 members. Through 2013, all inductees except one played some of their professional career in the NFL. The exception is Buffalo Bills guard Billy Shaw, the only player who played his entire career in the AFL prior to the 1970 merger.

Board of Selectors

Inductees are now selected by a 46-person committee largely made up of sportswriters. Normally the NFL team's beat writer for the major newspaper in that city has voting privileges. There are also 11 at-large delegates (usually from cities that lose an NFL team and are not granted an expansion team) and one representative from the Pro Football Writers Association. Except for the PFWA rep, who is appointed to a two-year term, the appointments are open-ended and terminated only by death, retirement or resignation.

Voting Procedure

- The player or coach must have been retired at least five years. Contributors such as a team owner or executive can be voted in at any time.
- Fans must nominate.
- The selection committee is polled three times (every three months) by mail to eventually narrow the list to 25 semifinalists. In November, the committee selects 15 finalists by mail balloting.
- Nine members of what is known as the "Seniors Committee" screen candidates who finished their career 25 years or more years prior. The committee adds two finalists from that group, which make a final ballot of 17 members.
- The Selection committee then meets the day before each Super Bowl game to elect a new class.

- To be elected, a finalist must receive at least 80 percent support from the board, with at least four, but no more than seven, candidates being elected annually.

Pro Football Hall of Fame 1996 Ballot

Name	Position	From	To	All-Pro	Pro Bowls	Starts	Games
Mel Renfro	DB	1964	1977	1 '71	10	13 yrs	174

Renfro waited 14 years after he became eligible to be on the ballot, which meant it was an agonizing 19 years of despair. Seven defensive players, arguably with similar or less credentials, received the necessary 80 percent of the vote to gain induction during that period.

Defensive back	Enshrined	Career	Years	Wait
Herb Adderley	1980	1961–71	12	5+3
Lem Barney	1992	1967–77	11	5+10
Mel Blount	1989	1970–83	14	5+4
Willie Brown	1984	1968–83	16	5+1
Jimmy Johnson	1994	1961–72	16	5+13
Dick Lane	1974	1952–65	14	5+4
Emlen Tunnell	1967	1948–61	14	5+1

The Ray Nitschke Luncheon

"I remember the luncheon well," said Mel. "Ray Nitschke getting into our face: 'Do you know what it means to be here?'"

The luncheon the day before the induction ceremony is attended only by living members and new inductees. Ray Nitschke, the first Packer to be inducted in the Pro Hall of Fame, always spoke at the luncheon. He always told inductees what a great honor they were receiving, that they were now members of the greatest team of them all. Following his death in 1998, the Hall named the luncheon after him.

Renfro Family Collection

Introduction and Acceptance Speeches

Jim Johnson:

> Tom Landry, who was elected to the Hall of Fame in 1990, was the Dallas Cowboys head coach from 1960 to 1988. Four players who played a majority of their careers under Coach Landry are already enshrined into the Hall. Today, Tom is here to present another Dallas Cowboy enshrinee, Mel Renfro. Please welcome Tom Landry.

Tom Landry:

Thank you very much. My congratulations to all of the recipients who will be joining Mel Renfro, who is being inducted into the Pro Football Hall of Fame. Of course when I came, I thought I was just going to induct him in here. I didn't know I was coming for a Redskin pep rally, but we had a lot of fun together. Though you have to admit, one of the pleasures of coaching to me is to have the privilege of coaching a player of Mel's outstanding ability. You could place Mel Renfro in any skilled position on a football field and you would have a Pro Bowl player.

He was born in Houston, Texas, which makes him a little special. He and his family eventually moved to Portland, Oregon, where he enjoyed outstanding athletic success both in football and track at Jefferson High School.

The Cowboys had their eye on Mel from the start. We knew he was going to be an outstanding pro and first round d pick. An off-the-field incident in 1963 almost ended Renfro's football career. President Kennedy was assassinated two weeks before the draft. When Renfro heard the disastrous news, he banged his fist on a mirror and severed a nerve in his hand. Like other NFL teams we weren't too sure if the nerve would be okay. So we took a calculated risk and picked a defensive tackle in the first round, hoping that Mel would last until the second. And boy, were we lucky that he did. Renfro had a spectacular rookie season in 1964 in three different categories, as a pass defender, a punt returner and a kickoff returner. We first played him as a free safety and he saved us many touchdowns with his speed. Naturally, Mel wanted to play offense. So in 1966, I put him at tailback and changed our offense. Unfortunately, he was injured on his ankle in the first ballgame. And before he got back in I put him back on defense because that is where I needed him anyway. Renfro is one of pro football's premier defensive backs by winning All-NFL acclaim in 1965, 1969, 1971, and 1973. All-NFL honors three times. He was selected to play in ten straight Pro Bowl games. He played in four Super Bowls and eight NFL and NFC championship games. He played with the Cowboys for fourteen seasons. Longer than any other, except Ed "Too Tall" Jones. And even with all his success, Mel was a team player. That is really what football is all about. And it is really a great, great pleasure for me to present Mel Renfro for induction into the 1996 Pro Football Hall of Fame.

Mel Renfro:

Thank you very much, Coach Landry. I would like to congratulate the other inductees. It really is a great honor to be standing here with all these fine men. I can honestly say that I wasn't sure that this day would ever arrive. I was eligible for fourteen years. When each year went by, my friends would say, you'll make it next year, Mel. Now I have made it at the last second and I am so very thankful.

I must tell you this seems to have happened to me before in the early years of the Dallas Cowboys. In 1967, 1968, and 1969 we lost to the Green Bay Packers twice, then the Cleveland Browns in championship games. I remember those long, lean years. We were always labeled as next year's champions. And there were times when we couldn't even go to a grocery store, where someone would recognize us and we would hear those snide remarks. Those so and so Cowboys can't win anything, can't win the big game, always losing. Our kids at school would get it. It was a tough time. In 1970, we finally won the big game to get us into the Super Bowl, but we lost to Baltimore in a last-second field goal by Jim O'Brien. It was heart-breaking. Then the next year we finally, finally came back to win it all. That championship involved a lot of hard work...A lot of blood, sweat, and a lot of tears. The credit then belongs to my teammates and coaches. The credit today belongs to my parents, my teachers, my coaches, my teammates, my family, and my friends.

As a child I was fortunate. My parents grounded me in the church. They taught me right from wrong and they taught me to believe in the Ten Commandments. There were many other people who were inspirational to me along the way. I remember my fifth-grade school teacher, Mrs. Lee Honeywell. She pulled me aside when I was ten years old and she said, "I see something special in you, Melvin. One day you are going to be someone." I didn't know what she meant. Oh, I knew I could run a little faster than some of the other kids, but she saw in me a vision...a vision of a professional athlete. She encouraged me to stay in the right path. I never heard from her or saw her again after grade school. One thing I want to say to her today is thank you. And Mrs. Honeywell, if you are out there, please call me. I took her words to heart and I stuck with athletics.

Tom DeSylvia was my football coach for three years in high school. We were 34 and one. He was like a second father to me. I remember his great halftime speech. He simply said, "Go out, reach down as far as you can reach...block and tackle and have fun." I went on to college. My football coach was Len Casanova. He helped us as much off the field as on the field. Teaching us solid work ethics, encouraging us to do things we need to do as men. And what can I say about Coach Landry that hasn't already been said. A fine Christian man. He was able to blend and work well in dealing with a secular organization and secular players. Tom Landry is a great teacher. We soon came to realize that if we had faith in him, played where he wanted us to play, did what he wanted us to do, that we would be successful. In retrospect, many years later as I was reading scripture I saw Coach Landry's methods. All the time he was training and teaching he was doing it from principles in the Bible. He was never threatening. And he never mentioned Christian principles or beliefs, but that is what it was. I know it now. I thank God for all these wonderful people who touched me throughout my life and I thank them too.

I grew up in the inner city in Portland, Oregon. I lived on the edge of the city where blacks were situated. I witnessed racial problems there when I was growing up, but it wasn't as bad as some places. When I went out to play for the Cowboys, I kept going back to Portland. I saw the community continue to deteriorate, year after year, when I always thought it would get better. By the time I retired from the NFL, it was not the same, drugs and the like. At the time, I tried to find a way to help my community, but I couldn't find anyone to help me. And I didn't know how to do it myself. I couldn't get it done. So I wandered, depressed and frustrated, I wandered. I went to Los Angeles for a year or two. I went to St. Louis for a year or two. I went to Las Vegas for a year or two. All the time I was thinking about Portland and something would always draw me back home. Well, now I am trying to do something for the youth of this nation. After all, they are our future. When the governments and schools can't cope, it is the time for the rest of us to pitch in. Athletes need to be role models. We need to present an image to people who want to do the right thing. Devoted to family, community, and church. To live honorable lives with ethics, integrity, with grace.

Today I have a goal. A ministry. We are going to build the biggest, finest Christian community center that anyone has seen in a long time. We are going to have arts and entertainment. An athletic facility that will attract people from all over the world and much, much more. We are going to bring Christian athletes to run clinics. To speak with the young kids who don't have any hope. We are going to teach ethics. We are going to give them hope. We are going to tell them that we see something special in each and every one. We will begin in Portland and call it the Bridge Center.

In Genesis 3:9 the Lord called to the man, "Where are you?" The man was always running, ducking, and hiding. In Hebrews 11 and 12, they called them great men of faith. They went through many trials. Samson and even Moses tried to get away from what God wanted them to do. They doubted. Jonah, he wandered. It took them a long time to be elevated to do the Lord's work. They thought they were ready sooner, but they weren't. God taught them. Gave them the

> lessons to wait, to be patient, to learn and their time would come. And that is what happened to me after I retired from football. I was carrying a lot of baggage. I just wandered. But the Lord was calling, "Where are you?" God had timing for me. But the Lord was saying, "You will make it next year, Mel." Go back to the Super Bowl after a while away. Go back home after a while away. Go back to religion after a while away. And now, back to the NFL after a while away. I feel now that I am ready. I wasn't ready before. It wasn't time, but it is now. And now here I am. I can't tell you how much this means to me. The glory and the credit are not mine today. The glory belongs to God. The credit belongs to my parents, teachers, coaches, my teammates, my family, and my friends. Go back after a while away and give back. Thank you very much.

Mrs. Lee Honeywell

Mel's plea to connect with his fifth-grade teacher was answered. Ken Wheeler of the *Oregonian* reported the following week: "Lee Honeywell is 90, lives in Sun City, California, and said she 'nearly dropped my teeth' Sunday morning when a friend in Medford called and gave her the news.

"The friend told her of Mel Renfro's reference to her in his speech Saturday while being inducted into the Pro Football Hall of Fame at Canton, Ohio – how he had credited her, his fifth-grade teacher, with being an influence on his life, and he wished to thank her and hoped to hear from her. 'I was teaching at Boise School. I had a room of 43 students and the room was built for 25. I loved those little devils, and they were little devils. We had a lot of fun in that class.

"'Besides that, I used to take my little girl, Jackie, to the parent-teacher meetings, and Mel would be there with his parents. He'd spend the whole time chasing her around. It makes you feel awfully big when somebody comes back years later and tells you that you influenced their lives to the best. It makes you kind of glow all over.'"

Within the month, Mel, energized with the location of his former teacher and his after-glow from the Hall of Fame event, jumped in his white Bridge Ministry van and drove from Dallas to Sun City to visit her for a couple of hours. It was pleasing for him to "close-the-loop" on that heart-felt part of his childhood memories...

"Football Heaven"

Hall-of-Famer Chris Carter calls it: "The greatest hall of all the halls," and to be in "Football Heaven" was the greatest day of his life. August 3, 2013, was the 50th Anniversary celebration for the Pro Football Hall of Fame at Canton, Ohio. A record 105 of the Hall's inductees showed up for the ceremony. The seven inductees brought to 280 the number of players, coaches and others that had been elected since the Hall was opened in 1963, representing the 23,000 that have played the sport at the professional level to that point. There have been a total of 15 defensive backs enshrined. Since Renfro was inducted in 1996, Mike Haynes, Mel Krause, Ronnie Lott, Darrell Green, Roger Wehrli, Emmitt Thomas and Dion Sanders have been honored. Former Baltimore Raven Jonathon Ogden, age 39, was the youngest player ever enshrined while ex-Green Bay linebacker Dave Robinson, age 73, waited 38 years after his retirement. Robinson called it "the closest thing to immortality. It gives me joy and inspiration that will last me the rest of my life."

Renfro Family Collection

Reunion of Doomsday I backs
Mel, Cornell Green Cliff Harris and Herb Adderley

28

Return to Dallas

SINCE MEL RENFRO'S STAR SHINED BRIGHTER IN DALLAS THAN IN Portland, Mel moved back to Dallas in 1996 before his induction in the Pro Football Hall of Fame. Upon his return, he reclaimed his legendary Cowboy image in Texas, where many doors opened for him to be independent and financially productive.

"Mary Knox of PPI, the talent marketing company, who handled the speaking engagements for Roger Staubach, Randy White and Tony Dorsett, contacted me," said Mel. "She said, 'Mel, you need to come down to Dallas. We will add you to our list.'" (Personalities & Promotions International, known as PPI, was a marketing company founded by Staubach.)

In Texas, Mel found so many requests for appearances that he opened his own small office and hired a full-time assistant in North Dallas to manage his new business affairs. "The first year and a half, I was making $15,000 to $25,000 a month doing a lot of appearances, autograph signings, speaking at luncheons, and doing small endorsements," said Mel. "I was even asked to visit the Army bases in Germany. I would also participate in 20 to 30 golf tournaments a year from Dallas to Portland, to New York, to Miami, and to LA – mostly fund-raisers for other Hall of Fame football players. I operated my own foundation and golf tournament in Dallas for five years before the year-round operation became too much for me to handle."

In addition, Mel said, "There are 15 of us 'Cowboy legends' who help owner Jerry Jones promote Cowboy football. It is usually a four-game stint a year at AT&T Stadium where we offer free pictures and autographs in the marketing suites for those who purchase season tickets in the VIP section."

Presently, Renfro has an on-line company he operates out of his home for autographed photographs.

The Bridge

Mel Renfro's vision to duplicate his Portland efforts for a youth center in Dallas fell short before he could get the program off the ground.

"I attempted to start my own Bridge Center in Dallas as I had done in Portland," said Mel. "It was called the Mel Renfro Bridge Foundation. The mission statement was the same as the Portland ministry, to build a Christian-based Center to help disadvantaged kids to have a safe haven."

But in Dallas, Renfro didn't secure a church connection. In the early stages when he was in the fund-raising mode to buy acreage east of Dallas, the project bogged down due to conflicts of interest. The investors Mel dealt with did not have the same heart for the project as Mel had. Their interest was solely on the financial return on their investment. Realizing their differences, Mel gave up his youth center plan. Nevertheless, Mel still supports non-profits who raise funds for those at-risk kids by doing a few events each year.

The Starfish Foundation of Dallas

In 1999, Renfro received a call from Belita Nelson, founder of the "Starfish Foundation of Dallas." Nelson had a son going through addiction.

"She asked my help," said Mel. "She needed a recognizable name to give the foundation some credibility. The program worked with kids with substance abuse. I took over the public relations and became the marketing director and board president for the Starfish Foundation for nearly six years. We counseled drug addicts and their families. Later we also became an awareness group after former Dallas Cowboy lineman Mark Tuinei died of an overdose." The foundation closed in 2005.

The experience was useful for Mel. Shortly after his service with Starfish he was prepared to accept a challenge of his own. An extended family member needed desperate help and Mel volunteered.

Mel was the godfather for niece Candice Renfro, the daughter of his late brother Raye and wife Virginia. Candice was in trouble and needed her uncle's help. She needed to leave her living situation in Vancouver, Washington, and receive intervention for her drug addiction.

Candice, in her late 20s, came to live at Mel's Dallas home to "dry out" in an effort to change her lifestyle. The Starfish Foundation provided Mel with sufficient information to deal with her issues toward a successful rehabilitation. Mel is proud of her success. "With a new environment, Candice found a job, she got her children back, she remarried, and now she's become a good functioning recovered-addict," said Mel.

Tom Landry's Services – February 12, 2000

In the opening chapter of *Landry: The Legend and the Legacy,* author Bob St. John was at his finest as he sensitively reflected the reactions of close friends, former players and teammates, Billy Graham, and the renowned Texas theologians and pastors who participated at the invitation-only private funeral and burial service at Sparkman/Hillcrest Funeral Home and Memorial Park in North Dallas, the memorial service at the Highland Park United Methodist Church and the public tribute at the Myerson Symphony Center in downtown Dallas.

Tom Landry Jr. asked Mel to join Charlie Waters, Drew Pearson, Pettis Norman, Tony Dorsett, Bob Lilly, Randy White, and Dan Reeves to carry the casket from the hearse to the gravesite. Bob Hayes, somewhat overcome with emotion, also joined them.

Marriage

When Mel returned to Dallas in 1996, he ran into Elizabeth "Liz" Salas, an early acquaintance from the 1980s, at Walmart. While he was working and selling beer products at Miller, Mel developed a relationship with her future husband, an African safari hunter, and subsequently was invited to their wedding. "When they got married," remembers Mel, "her brother, the best man, didn't show up. So I stood in for him."

"After Landry passed, Liz saw me on TV and gave me a call," said Mel. "Her first husband had died, she got remarried, but it didn't work out and now she was divorced. We dated and got married in 2001."

Liz, 17 years younger than Mel, is a native Dallasite. She has three grown children: two daughters, Michelle and Tara, and a son Chris. She is also a grandmother to Shelby, Riley, Anna, "Teddy" and Marshall.

Liz has worked with software, been a housewife, a mother, has home-schooled kids and is presently a busy real estate agent. The bonus for her home sales is an autographed Dallas Cowboy football and a personal picture with her legendary husband – Super Bowl rings and all.

Renfro's 55-year friend and mentor Cowboy executive Gil Brandt says, "She has been a good match for Mel. Liz has stabilized him."

"Liz supports me through my health issues," says Mel. "She also watches my back and has kept me out of a lot of jams. We are both

Christians and have learned to lean on each other a lot. We attend Tony Evans' mega church – The Oak Cliff Bible Fellowship."

Prostate Cancer

In 2002, Renfro was in New Jersey for a casino fundraiser when he got a phone call from his doctor's office: 'Mel, we got your blood tests back, and you need to come to see us. There is nothing to worry about.'"

But there was concern. Mel's elevated PSA (Prostate Specific Antigen) numbers required referral to a urologist for possible prostate cancer. Two biopsies of the prostate gland produced a Gleason No. 9 score – a high diagnostic staging number that recognized an aggressive cancer. The Gleason number is the sum of two of the most involved biopsies.

"I was sitting down when they told me," said Mel. "My heart seemed to drop. I was afraid for the first time in my life. 'How long do I have to live?' I thought. I had to realize that life can be short."

Mel dealt with his anxiety. "I'm a tough cookie," he said. "I told myself, 'Get a grip on this. I want to live life to its fullest.'"

Within a week, Mel Renfro had a prostatectomy at Doctors Hospital in Dallas. To his well-being, his cancer was contained within the capsule of the prostate gland.

In 2009, seven years later, the doctors noticed a rise in Mel's PSA. The secondary treatment required six weeks of focused low-dosage radiation. Despite some localized skin damage from the radiation, his PSA score remains at 0.

Although there are ongoing controversies concerning the benefit of prostate cancer screening and treatment of localized disease, prostate cancer continues to be the second most common cause of cancer deaths among men in the United States.

Scientists do not understand why prostate cancer incidence

and death rates are higher within the African-American population. "Black men are more likely to be to be diagnosed with prostate cancer, are diagnosed at a younger age, display larger tumors and are more than twice as likely to die from prostate cancer that has spread throughout the body than white males," said Dr. Isla Garraway, a prostate researcher at UCLA.

To address the need for early diagnosis, The Methodist Health Systems utilized Renfro as their spokesman for the Dallas community screenings for prostate cancer for three years. He was used in a number of ways to tell his story. The video on their website is both impressive and effective. The hospital director claims they save over 40 lives a year through their screening.

2004 – Hall of Fame Mortgage Company

The Hall of Fame Mortgage Company hired both Tony Dorsett and Mel Renfro in 2004 as marketing tools. "We were used specifically as personal relation people for the business," reported Mel. "We were there until they closed in 2008."

29

Family Legacy

Mel Renfro feels blessed that he shares a mutual and healthy adult relationship with each of his four children.

The oldest three were raised by their single parent mother after Mel and Pat separated in 1974. Melvin was 10, Tony nine and

Photo by Bob Gill

Mel Jr, Mel, Cynthia, Tony, and wife Liz

Cynthia six when mother Pat downsized their home and went to work in Portland while Mel stayed in Dallas pursuing his football career with the Cowboys. They divorced in 1976.

Jason, the youngest, was born in 1981 in Dallas to Mel and his second wife, Mechelle Simmons. Jason had a different childhood experience than the older three; he was raised by a single father, his dad, when he was handed off to Mel at five. "Raising Jason at that time of my life gave me a purpose and stabilized me," said Mel. "He became my little 'buddy.' He went everywhere with me."

Melvin Lacey Renfro, Jr., 1-25-1964

Melvin was a top soccer player in the Rockwood youth program and continued playing the game through his sophomore year in high school before he turned to football. He became a star running back on Coach Craig Ruecker's Reynolds 1980–81 league championship teams which lost only three games in two years.

One of the few times Mel got to see son Melvin play was at a playoff football game. "Right after I got seated for the kickoff," remembered Mel, "Melvin returned it all the way for a touchdown. I got so excited, I jumped up and screamed."

Melvin won the long jump state championship in 1982. His season personal best was 24-1, a quarter-inch short of his dad's state record of 22 years earlier. The effort earned him a track scholarship to the University of Oregon. But Melvin hyper-extended his knee early in his first year, which aborted his college career.

After a few years of job-hopping, Melvin took a three-week vacation to Italy, which determined he loved to travel. He applied to the airlines for work. Since, he has traveled the world. Melvin recently transferred back to Portland to be around family and friends. "Never married," he says. No kids."

"I always had a great relationship with Dad," said Melvin. "I visit him in Dallas a few times each year for the last six years."

Anthony "Tony" Patrick Renfro, 3-29-1965

Tony's high school athletic career shifted to track and field after trying out football. "I decided I didn't like getting hit in the head being a running back," said Tony. "So I decided I would run track and field." He went to the state meet both his junior and senior years in the triple jump, long jump and both relays.

Tony worked for Nike for 10 years in the team sports department, before he took a job with Capital One as a fraud investigator the next 15 years. Tony is divorced with two daughters, Madison, 20, and Shelby, 18.

Tony remembers the freedom his brother and he had running up and down the Cowboy practice field sidelines while his dad was practicing. "I always looked forward to the tons of donuts in the locker room and how well we were treated by everyone," said Tony. "I have great memories and I'm very proud to be the son of a professional football player and I'm a Dallas Cowboy for life!"

Cynthia Renée Renfro, 3-14-1968

Mel expected his daughter to have athletic skills, but he is in awe of her other talents, her instincts, her aptitude and her personal drive to find a career niche. "Cynthia's my A student," he says.

"I love my Pops," said Cynthia, Mel's 47-year-old daughter. "He is the only father figure I ever had in my life. There was a rough period when we didn't see much of Dad for years at a time. Now it has been a delight to be able to spend time with him and know he is well taken care of."

Cynthia was very active in sports in school. Her mother got her started in gymnastics before she branched into soccer and track and field. When Cynthia graduated from high school, she had two options for college: accepting an athletic scholarship to the University of Pacific or, as a Merit Scholar, accepting a full academic scholarship for the college of her choice. She chose USC, but after a year of cultural shock, transferred to UCLA, where she finished with a degree in history. Her own "My adventure" story led her to many stops, working with Ralph Nader and the Ted Turner Family Foundation, before she settled on philanthropy as a career. After working for the Marguerite Casey Foundation for nine years, Cynthia started her own consulting business in Seattle in 2012. She has never married.

Jason Raye Renfro, 10-16-1981

Renfro Family Collection

Son Jason with Mel 2015

Jason, the youngest, has memories of being treated special by his single parent father, be it a birthday bike, ninja turtles, or a dog named "Robocop." At 10, he remembers the move to Las Vegas and learning to play pool at the sports lounge as "Little Fro."

"When Dad met and married Evett," said Jason. "I suddenly had siblings. We were now a family of five, and I being the youngest got hassled and picked on. But I had people to laugh, play and fight with. The best thing was my step-mom. During that time, she taught me how to cook and clean for myself. She is and always will be special to me."

"When the whole family went to Canton for the Hall of Fame induction," said Jason, "I didn't realize how big a deal it was. I kept thinking, man, my dad sure is sweating a lot, and I've never seen so many people in one place before."

When Jason got married, his dad toasted him at the reception. "The only thing I can remember his saying is how proud he was of me," said Jason. "Everything after that was white noise. My dad speaking on my behalf just made the day even more memorable."

"I've been married to Melissa for seven years," said Jason. "We have two amazing kids, Jai, and Jaxon. My wife is a godsend, an incredible woman. My mom [Mechelle] and I have a good relationship and our kids love their 'Gigi' as she likes to be called. I'm currently doing modeling and acting.

"I know the public sees Dad as a football legend," said Jason. **"What I see is a man who did his best he could to raise a son on his own, which to me is more heroic than any physical feat."**

30

Health and NFL Settlement

Today, the man whom Cowboy teammates know as "Bro Fro" exercises by walking daily for 30 to 40 minutes around a local park in his Dallas neighborhood. "I feel blessed," said Mel Renfro. "My doctors tell me my vitals are good. My heart is good and I don't have any kidney problems."

NFLPA Lawsuit

Hundreds of lawsuits have been filed in the last 20 years by former players with long-term cognitive issues. The NFL has downplayed them during their negotiations with the league's players association to compensate players for injuries suffered while playing.

On April 22, 2015, Federal District Court Judge Anita Brody agreed on a settlement with the NFL and players association to increase the available money for the 90 or so concussion-affected retired players. Those who qualify will have the opportunity to receive benefits or to opt out (the option to sue independently). Age and timing is such that Mel will apply for his benefits. He has done the due diligence by undergoing a battery of tests and examinations.

Concussions

An important part of Renfro's medical history is the nine brain concussions he suffered playing the sport he loved. "I had three in high school, three in college and three in the pros," said Mel. "But I would do it over again."

Quite a testimony for the 73-year-old whose history of trauma and surgical repair still causes lingering pain and debilitating issues and would suggest otherwise.

Mel pieced together a game crisis in Philadelphia following a tackle in 1965 as a run-stopping safety: "I was sitting alone on the end of the bench for I don't know for how long, maybe 60 seconds – struggling to collect myself. It was an odd experience. 'Who am I and where am I?' Then after a bit, I looked up at the scoreboard. 'OK, I am at a football game.' Then after another 20 seconds or so, I suddenly woke up. 'I'm Mel Renfro sitting on the sidelines of a football game.' I didn't have any treatment or any follow-up evaluation."

Roger Staubach

Fortune Magazine documented Roger Staubach's concussion story: He had one in high school, one in college at Navy, six in the NFL, maybe 20 total if you count the dings. L.C. Greenwood delivered one, and so did Earl Robinson, and Ray Nitschke. In Staubach's last game against the Los Angeles Rams in 1979, Jack Reynolds, a beast of a linebacker called Hacksaw, bounced his head like a basketball dribble off the turf. Staubach threw one subsequent pass to an offensive guard. Staubach had his first CT scan after that game and the doctor recommended that he retire.

Chronic Traumatic Encephalopathy (CTE)

In an interview in 2015, Tony Dorsett discussed his diagnosis of having signs of CTE, a degenerative brain condition that can only be confirmed accurately postmortem. The condition caused by head trauma can lead to dementia and depression. The 60-year-old Dorsett has opted out of the settlement wanting his case to stand on its own when he files it.

Dorsett ran for 12,738 yards over his 12 years with the Cowboys and of course, took many hits. He remembers a helmet-to-helmet he took in a 1984 game that knocked him out. He called it the hardest hit he ever took. Today, his concern is what the future holds for him. He forgets often and is noticeably short-tempered with family members.

The largest number of athletes suffering from CTE comes from the contact sports of football, ice hockey, rugby, boxing and wrestling. Others are people involved in the military service, and those with a history of previous chronic seizures, domestic violence and other activities resulting in repetitive head collisions.

CTE is a condition whereby the protein substance called tau builds up in the brain from repeated head trauma. It is diagnosed by examining cross-sections taken from several regions of the brain. The test takes months to complete and costs thousands of dollars.

Clinical symptoms of CTE are only beginning to be understood. They are thought to include changes in mood (i.e., depression, suicidality, apathy, anxiety), cognition (i.e., memory loss, excessive dysfunction), behavior (short fuse and aggression), and in some cases motor disturbance (i.e., difficulty with balance and gait).

Since 2008, the Sports Legacy Institute joined with the Boston University School of Medicine to form the Center for the Study of Traumatic Encephalopathy (CSTE). The Brain Injury Research Institute (BIRI) also studies the impact of concussions. They are currently the state-of-the-art in the field.

As of December 2012, the bodies of 33 former professional football players had undergone postmortem evaluations for CTE, and **all of them showed evidence of the disease.** Some are:

- Steeler legendary center Mike Webster, after a change of personality, died at age 50.
- Ex-Steeler lineman Terry Long drank antifreeze to commit suicide at age 36.
- Eagles DB Andre Waters committed suicide at age 44.
- Steeler Justin Strzelczyk, after the 36-year-old didn't resemble the fellow his friends and family knew, crashed his pickup truck at 100 MPH after a 31-mile chase the wrong way on New York's deadliest toll road.
- Active Kansas City linebacker Jovan Belcher, at age 25 murdered his girlfriend and committed suicide in front of the Chiefs' GM.
- Lou Creekmur, at age 82 died of dementia, the most advanced case of CTE to date.
- Houston linebacker John Grimsley died at 45 from an accidental gunshot.
- Tom McHale, a Houston Oiler linebacker, died at 45 from a drug overdose.
- Bengal wide receiver Chris Henry at age 26, fell out of the back of a moving truck.
- Dave Duerson, the Chicago Bear DB, after suffering from dementia took his life at 50 with a self-inflicted gunshot.
- Buffalo Bills running back Cookie Gilchrist, who ran harder than anyone in the American Football League, died at 75. Researchers found he had CTE disease in Stage IV, the most advanced category. From age 35, he demonstrated the clinical picture of having CTE, difficulties in behavior and cognition, with the most striking in the last several decades.
- John Mackey, the star of Baltimore's Blooper Bowl win, died at 69 of dementia after receiving $88,000 a year and $50,000

for day care (the NFL's 88 plan – for his number) to pay for his last four years in the nursing home.

- Charger great and a 20-year veteran of the NFL Junior Seau, at age 43, suffering from mood changes and irritability, died in 2012 from a self-inflicted gunshot. (The Seau children are opting out of the class-action suit. They feel the monetary rewards are insufficient.)
- Former Atlanta Falcon Ray Easterling shot himself at age 62 after struggling with dementia.
- Wally Hilgenberg, the Viking linebacker through 16 seasons and four Super Bowls died in 2008 at age 66 with a preliminary diagnosis of Lou Gehrig's disease. His brain was studied postmortem finding CTE as the official diagnosis.

In the 2015 off-season, a number of NFL players have retired early with concussion or another health risk as possible motives, four of them 30 or younger: Chris Borland, Pat Willis, Jake Locker, and Jason Worilds.

Chris Borland, a 25-year-old former Wisconsin All-American linebacker who made over 100 tackles in a 10-game span his rookie year with the 49ers in 2014, walked away from at least $2.35 million when he abruptly retired from the NFL. Borland estimated he has suffered over 30 concussions since he was 14 years old. He wasn't willing to risk his present health further by enduring "a thousand or 1500 hits every fall for the next 10 years."

Since the science is still limited on concussions, there is a pending application for a $17 million CTE study funded by the NFL through the National Institutes of Health.

Painkillers

Mel Renfro was also one of 13 plaintiffs of former NFL players that have filed a lawsuit on May 21, 2015, claiming all 32 NFL teams, their doctors, trainers and medical staffs obtained and provided pain-killers to players, often illegally, as part of a decades-long conspiracy to keep them on the field without regard for their long-term health.

The lawsuit filed in the U.S. Northern District of Maryland alleges intentional activity by the teams, not negligence. It's a part of a unified effort to provide health care and compensation to the thousands of former players and their families who have been permanently injured or died as a result of playing professional football.

Pain management continues to be a day-to-day problem. Mel had his left hip replaced in 2008, spinal stenosis surgery in 2014 and double carpal-tunnel surgery in 2015. He has serious bone spurs, neuropathic issues, arthritis and problems with his balance. He needs weekly physical therapy. He doesn't play golf at celebrity fundraisers. He rides the cart and his play is limited to putting.

Unlike the high school and college football players of today, Mel was always a two-way player. He never came off the field. "I was always running and catching the football on offense, making tackles and defending passes on defense, returning kicks and punts," said Mel.

In college at Oregon, Mel missed eight games. A chipped bone in his right ankle against Utah during his sophomore season forced him to miss four games; a broken rib his senior season kept him out two games; and a wrist-slash home accident ended his college career a week before the Civil War game and the Sun Bowl.

Renfro played in the NFL for 14 seasons before a right leg injury forced his retirement. He had cartilage removed in 1977. He survived in a league in which his teammates and opponents were the biggest, the fastest and the strongest in the game.

The first five years were brutal on Mel's body before Coach Landry extended his career by moving him from the physical, run-stopping safety position to the cornerback position, where he excelled as one of NFL's top shut-down defenders, thus reducing the blows his body absorbed.

Being pragmatic about playing football with its consequences, Mel said in a 2011 *Dallas Cowboys Star Magazine* interview: "Football is a physical game. It's a collision sport, and you're going to have some problems later on in life. I look at the game nowadays and I see those guys hitting the way they hit and all that, and I just feel sorry for them, because 15 to 20 years from now, they are going to suffer. I mean, it's not a matter of *if*, it's a matter of *when*, because the body wasn't designed to play football. So you are going to hurt."

Postscript

When Mel was asked how he would like to be remembered, he said: "Mel Renfro always gave his best." He deflected to his father's early encouragement. "As a young child my Dad would see me struggling, he would say softly, 'Son, just do the best you can.' That carried over to me in school, sports, family and work. I look back on my life and feel proud of my accomplishments. A big thanks to my dad and all those who encouraged me along the way."

31

Renfro Honors and Halls of Fame

1959 Wigwam Wiseman H.S. Football All-American

1960 Governor's Trophy – Golden West Invitational. "Top high school track athlete of the year"

1960 Hopkin Jenkins Award – Outstanding athlete at Jefferson High

1960 Oregon Shrine High School All-Star Game – MVP

1962 Pigskin Club of Washington DC Trophy – Outstanding college back in America

1962 NCAA Track All-American

1962 Consensus Football All-American

1963 Football All-American

1963 Hoffman Award – University of Oregon outstanding player

1964, 1965, 1969, 1971, 1973 All-Pro – first team

1981 Cowboy Ring of Honor

1982 Portland Interscholastic League Hall of Fame

1983 State of Oregon Sports Hall of Fame

1986 National Football Foundation Hall of Fame

1990 Oregon Afro-American Athletic Hall of Fame

1992 University of Oregon Athletic Hall of Fame

1995 National High School Hall of Fame

1996 Texas Afro-American Athletic Hall of Fame

1996 Pro Football Hall of Fame

1998 State of Texas Sports Hall of Fame

2001 NFL Order of the Leather Helmet – Individual who made significant contributions to the game of pro football

Chapter Sources

Adderly, Herb and Dave Robinson, with Royce Boyles. *Lombardi's Left Side*. Olathe, KS: Ascend Books, 2012.

Boyles, Bob and Paul Guido. *50 Years of College Football.* New York: Skyhorse Publishing. 2007

Clark, Kristine Setting. *Bob Lilly, A Cowboy's Life*. Chicago: Triumph Books, 2008.

Clark, Kristine Setting. "The Allegations Stop Here," The Coffin Corner, 1996.

Golenbock, Peter. *Landry's Boys: An Oral History of a Team and an Era*. Chicago: Triumph Books, 2005.

Kirchman, Mark. *Willamette Week*. Feb. 23, 1982.

Kramer, Jerry. *Instant Replay*. New York: The World Publishing Co., 1968.

Landry, Tom and Gregg Lewis. *Tom Landry: An Autobiography*. New York: HarperCollins, 1990.

Moore, Kenny. *Bowerman and the Men of Oregon*. Emmaus, PA: Rodale, 2006.

Monk, Cody. *Legends of the Dallas Cowboys*. Champaign, IL: Sports Publishing LLC, 2004.

Multnomah County Library digitized Oregonian newspapers.

Patoski, Joe Nick. *The Dallas Cowboys*. New York: Little Brown and Company, 2012.

Pro Football Reference, www.pro-football-reference.com.

Smith, Don. *Mel Renfro*. The Coffin Corner, 1996.

St. John, Bob. *Landry, The Legend and The Legacy.* Nashville: Word Publishing, 2000.

Taylor, Jean-Jacques. *Dallas Morning News*. 1996 - HOF.

Sullivan, Jeff. *America's Team.* San Rafael, CA: Insight Editions, 2010.

Van Leuven, Hendrick. *Touchdown UCLA*. Texas: Strode Publishers, 1988.

Author Bio

Mel with author Bob Gill

Dr. Bob Gill, a retired dentist in Portland, Oregon, has been an avid football fan since his own playing days at Jefferson High School, Oregon State and Portland State. He developed an interest in Oregon sports history with his work with the State of Oregon Sports Hall of Fame. Since, he has authored ***It's In Their Blood,*** a book that honors the legacies of 53 Oregon football coaches, and many magazine articles. As a sports historian, Gill successfully nominated former Oregon State and UCLA coach Tommy Prothro in 1991, Portland State quarterback Neil Lomax in 1996, and Linfield coach Ad Rutschman in 1998 to the National Football Foundation's Hall of Fame. He has been active with the Portland chapter of the NFF for 40 years and as the game chairman for the Les Schwab Bowl, the annual high school all-star game, for the last 18 years. He lives in Milwaukie, Oregon.

CPSIA information can be obtained
at www.ICGtesting.com
Printed in the USA
LVOW04s2307041215
465428LV00002B/4/P